Hygge

Unlock the Danish Art of Coziness and Happiness

Contents

General Introduction

Cravings for comfort, coziness, and contentment: everyone experiences the desire for a happier, less stressful, and more serene life. Hygge, the Danish-born philosophy, is one proven way to achieve such a life. From the Old Norse for "well-being", hygge embodies a philosophy that is as much a mindset as it is a way of life with specific activities designed to encourage you to cultivate togetherness and joy at the smallest and simplest things in everyday life.

With this book, you will learn about the hygge lifestyle, with a philosophical overview of what hygge is and how it relates to overall happiness. The Danes have been voted happiest people on earth numerous times; surely, this homegrown philosophy has something of merit to recommend it. Also, within the book are many basic tips and ideas for how to practice hygge in your own life, from home décor and atmosphere to how you dress and spend your leisure time. There is also a hygge way of approaching food and entertainment, the holidays, and seasonal activities. Underlying it all, hygge continually emphasizes the spirit of togetherness, fostering relationships with family and friends, and nurturing yourself through self-care.

Simplicity and serenity go hand-in-hand to create an atmosphere of cozy comfort and genuine fellowship. So, go find yourself a pair of warm, woolen socks, a super-soft blanket, and curl up in a hyggekrog (cozy nook). Read on about how to immerse yourself in hygge, the Danish secret to a happier life!

Chapter 1 Introduction: What the Heck is Hygge?

Consistently ranked among the happiest - if not the most joyful - nations on earth, Denmark must be doing something right. All human beings crave comfort, security, and happiness; indeed, the pursuit of happiness is one of the defining motivations of modern life. The Danes seem to have stumbled upon a simple secret that the rest of us - with our busy, distracted lives - have missed. That little secret well-being might be a concept called *hygge*. Pronounced "hoo-gah," hygge describes a lifestyle filled with contentment, a kind of "coziness of the soul," according to Meik Wiking, the CEO of the Happiness Research Institute in Copenhagen. Hygge encompasses a wide range of attitudes, feelings, and activities that are designed for comfort and happiness in security and simplicity.

Where Does Hygge Come From?

Various sources suggest different origins for the word "hygge," though all agree that it has some relation to comfort and coziness. Most sources suggest that the word originated from the Norwegian - with whom the Danes shared a nation-state until the early nineteenth century. To Norwegians, it means "well-being." It is also translated from the Danish to mean "to give courage, comfort, joy," and it has become a defining characteristic of Danish culture, particularly in the last few years. In 2016, it was in the finals for "word of the year" according to the *Oxford English Dictionary*, and there has been an explosion of interest in the concept and lifestyle that it defines. One could speculate that the timing is no accident, given the uncertainties in international politics and the continuing growth of technology often perceived as alienating.

In another line of etymological thinking, hygge may be derived from the sixteenth-century word *hugge* which means "to embrace," which is also linked to the words *hygga*, meaning "to comfort," and *hugr*, meaning "mood." Whatever the exact origin of the term, hygge has come to mean a combination of all the above: a warm, embracing hug as a way of life.

What about those Woolen Socks?

Hygge is defined by numerous characteristics, from the way your home is decorated and lit to the comfort in your personal attire. In fact, lighting is one of the key components of implementing the hygge atmosphere into your life: more than three-quarters of Danes, when asked what they most associate with hygge, say "candles." From this, you can infer that one of the most important characteristics of hygge is the attention to home and hearth. Indeed, the emphasis on togetherness and social relationships is also key to hygge, and your hyggelige home should be warm and welcoming, with the soothing glow of candlelight.

Still, hygge is not merely about the comforts of home (though this is crucial); it is also about how you eat and drink, dress, and celebrate. Simple and hearty food, without too much fuss, is a hallmark of the hygge lifestyle. Hygge doesn't demand that you count calories obsessively or that you put too many nutritional expectations on yourself. Conversely, it doesn't indicate that you can indulge just for the sake of indulgence - that's not the hygge way. Instead, hygge embraces simple moderation combined with a sense of calm and comfort. Stew and porridge factor largely in the pleasures of hygge, along with warming drinks and general relaxation. A decent blanket and a pair of soothing woolen socks are must-haves for an evening in front of a fire, or the glow of a television set, not to eliminate all the trappings of modernity. A "Netflix and chill" evening may not be the most central tenant of hygge, though its aim is far off the mark! Clothing is comfortable and basic, practical, and cozy. Hygge is not about "seeing and being seen," or standing out in a crowd; it is a humble way of presenting yourself to the world, with your happiness illuminating you from the inside out. The same attitude applies to celebrations: celebrate with contentment and togetherness, embracing your gratitude toward all the little things that make up your good life.

Hygge and Mindfulness

Once you begin to embrace hygge, it becomes not only a style but also a mindset. It encourages you to see the world differently, not through what you can acquire or achieve but through how you can appreciate and take part in the *small joys of life*. As with the Eastern concepts of mindfulness and meditation, hygge encourages you to stay in the present, enjoying what you have with loved ones and spending your time qualitatively rather than quantitatively. Indeed, this may be one of the central components of the hygge lifestyle that defines the contemporary Danish understanding of happiness: decoupling the feelings of happiness and comfort from the trappings of wealth and status.

This is part of the idea of hygge, as well, which also emphasizes equality and teamwork, modesty and simplicity. Some criticize this spirit within the Scandinavian culture in general, suggesting that it encourages a kind of conformity long associated with various Northern European countries. This conformity welcomes the idea that no particular person should stand out or show off. While hygge may suggest an element of this thought, it by no means encourages it as the aim of the lifestyle. Rather, it encourages finding satisfaction in the everyday parts of life, promoting tolerance and togetherness that everyone should be a part of.

State-sponsored Hygge

The argument about what makes hygge so achievable in Danish life - and its similar cousins in other Nordic countries - lies within the success of the so-called "welfare state." Many of the financial burdens of middle-class life in Danish society are relieved via the state: universal health care, social security, free education at universities, plenty of paid family leave and generous paid vacation time, as well as a highly functional infrastructure. Thus, Danes can enjoy the small comforts of life and the inherent joys of family and friends because they are not ridden with anxiety over how to afford a decent, comfortable middle-class existence. That said, Danish taxes are quite high (especially when compared to America), hovering above 50 percent in personal income tax. Still, the Danes are quite willing to accept this tax rate in exchange for the excellent benefits. Their priorities center around investing in the quality of life and participating in the larger society, a kind of culture of national togetherness - something other Western countries might seriously consider.

Hygge is most definitely associated with a level of financial security and economic mobility that many other places and peoples in the world do not have. This is part of what makes the practice of hygge special in its attributes - but rare in its attainability.

The spirit of hygge emphasizes humility in its practice. Having a secure social system and a stable infrastructure provides great assistance in attaining the highest levels of hyggelige. Still, regardless of the availability of that assistance, you can indulge in the daily mindset of embracing the simplicity of every day, the comforting and familial of nearly any circumstance. Again, hygge is not merely a set of rules;' it is a mindset devoted to engaging with daily life in a present, mindful, and positive manner.

The Most Hyggelige Time of the Year

Unsurprisingly, wintertime (especially Christmas) is when hygge is intensely recognized and practiced by those in Nordic lands. The reasons are numerous: in a harsh winter climate, it makes perfect sense to bask in the warm comforts of cozy, woolen socks and gently roaring fires, wrapped in a blanket in a candlelit room. Foods and drinks most associated with a hygge lifestyle are also all about warming comfort: porridges, and stews and mulled wines. These are all welcome distractions from the raging winter weather outside - and more than that, they are all reminders of how our own little pocket of daily life is safe and warm, cozy, and comforting. We create a shelter from all of life's storms.

This is not to say that hygge cannot be practiced year-round – of course, it should - but it also acknowledges that festive spirit that comes with most winter holidays. For many of us who celebrate Christmas, this festive spirit is quite familiar and very similar to many of the aspects of hygge itself. A hygge lifestyle is lived in this festive spirit, evoked throughout the year, encouraged by taking pleasure in intimate surroundings with our loved ones *every day*, not just snow days! Indeed, we would all be much happier looking forward to – and building our days around - an appreciation of daily life, togetherness, and cozy contemplation - no matter the time of year.

Practicing Hygge

So, now that you have a solid understanding of what hygge is and why it deserves careful consideration as a lifestyle, let's talk about how this can work for you in practical ways.

In the next chapter, we will examine the direct link between personal happiness and the practice of hygge: what is happiness, and how can hygge be a conduit to achieving it? Then, we will move on to exploring the practical ways in which we can integrate the concept of hygge into most aspects of our lives.

From the general attitude of employing hygge into our everyday lives to the fine details of how to practice particular parts of hyggelige, the rest of the book will look at specific elements of life in which hygge plays an important role. Creating a home environment that encourages and supports the mindset of hygge is key, as well as considering your personal dress and appearance; nothing too fussy, but certainly something lovely and comfortable. There are also tips and techniques - along with a handful of recipes - for cooking and consuming in the hygge style, with another chapter specifically focused on how to hygge up your holidays at any time of the year.

Following that, we will look at how hygge can increase our happiness by amplifying our familial relationships. Areas include using hygge in parenting, as well as bringing our loved ones together in positive ways for more sustained periods of time. We will also address the frugal nature of hygge; it is not a lifestyle that is based on conspicuous consumption and ambitious striving. Rather, it is a gentle, peaceful, and comfortable existence that can be achieved with little in the way of material struggling. Finally, we will spend some time looking at hygge-styled crafts and how we can engage in creating a cozier life with our own two hands.

Unlock this uniquely Danish art of living happily and cozily, embracing life with an open, warm hug, and engaging with your world in a mindful, humble manner. Happiness and well-being are only a few chapters away!

Chapter 2: How Hygge Helps Happiness

While it is our inalienable right to pursue happiness here in the US, too often it feels elusive considering our hectic, harried lifestyles and attachments to too many material things. Hygge may be one way to right that ship, supported with clear evidence from Denmark being consistently considered the happiest country on earth. Possibly, some guidance from the hygge lifestyle is just what we need to help guide us to greater happiness.

We all want bliss and happiness, and our ideas of that - and for that - vary from one person to another. For many of us, there are points in our life that disappoint; we thought we were on the path to happiness just to find we weren't even close to the right direction! We wind up very unhappy instead. Many studies have shown that people choosing to follow the high dollar, high-stress careers end up less content than peers who chose rewarding careers helping their fellow man - even if less financially lucrative. This is where a concept like hygge can come in and reframe our concepts of happiness. Instead of being defined by wealth and achievement, it may be marked by family togetherness and a contented home. If what we once thought we wanted has failed to bring happiness, then surely there are alternate ways of defining happiness. Hygge is demonstrably one of them, as people who practice it routinely report high levels of happiness and contentment.

Happiness as a destination for solely our personal fulfillment should not be the only thing driving us. Living a joyful life is also crucial to our overall health and well-being, emotionally and physically. The medical evidence keeps mounting: unhappiness is detrimental to our short-term needs and our long-term health. Among other things, it promotes heart health. People reporting happiness also report lower blood pressure and heart rates, both of which affect long-term heart health. It also boosts our immune systems; people who consistently maintained positive outlooks on their lives also consistently avoided colds and other minor ailments over time! In fact, happiness helps us to avoid pain in general - people who claim to be happy report far fewer aches and pains that many of us experience in our daily lives. The difference here may not be necessarily physical, but it is no less powerful to contemplate that our state of mind can alleviate physical pain itself. Other, more complicated diseases have shown to be less severe or to occur less often in people who reported spending a lot of time in social groups. Certainly, high levels of happiness are associated with low levels of stress, and we have all heard of how acutely damaging stress is to our physical well-being over time. Last, happy people often lead longer lives and are more productive well into their later years. The benefits of feeling happiness are undeniable, and, like hygge, this is a state of mind. The Danes are a great example of hygge in action!

Many wellness experts tout the benefits of the hygge lifestyle in its improvement over our emotional state of mind, our physical health, and our social well-being. Emotionally, one of the benefits of hygge is to promote a sense of calm and peacefulness. For example, if your home is cozy and comforting - with gentle candlelit rooms, warm furniture, blankets, and the smells of delicious home cooking - then it stands to reason that your state of mind is also at peace, not stressful. Other emotional benefits of hygge practice may include a decrease in depression - it's hard to stay depressed when you're comfortable and secure without much anxiety. Additionally, increased feelings of optimism and self-worth are often by-products of practicing hygge, as your state of mind will not be as linked to external desires and things that may be out of your control. This will also foster a sense of mindfulness and an appreciation for the little things in your life. Living a life filled with gratitude is certainly a sign of living a life filled with happiness.

As discussed above, practicing hygge in your life leads to physical health benefits. In addition to the emotional benefits, the physical benefits are just as important. Incorporating hygge into your daily routine can lead to a physically stronger life. For instance, hygge can improve sleep patterns - crucial to maintaining a sense of calm productivity. Within the security of a hygge space, external threats no longer loom large, and with that comfort comes better sleep, which leads to better self-care overall. It is difficult, for example, to exercise regularly and maintain a healthy weight if one is depressed, anxious, and lacking sleep. Also, some suggest that practicing hygge keeps you from overindulging in substances that allegedly help you cope with stress but can harm you physically, such as alcohol or other drugs.

Finally, there are also social benefits gained from practicing hygge. When we feel safe and comfortable, it becomes easier to reach out to others without feeling insecure and vulnerable. If we make our home welcoming and inviting to ourselves, it follows that others will find out home equally as alluring.

One of the fundamental concepts within hygge is that togetherness is truly part of the formula for overall happiness. Connecting with others is important both for our personal well-being and that of our community. This is an art that is being lost in the maze of technological devices and the distractions of our contemporary world. We may like using the word "communication" when discussing our beloved technology of texting or social media, yet our devices don't foster an authentic sense of connection. Hygge can help us to regain some of that feeling of connection. When a sense of security and comfort is established and maintained, we can then focus on increasing our trust in one another, ultimately creating a greater sense of intimacy within our relationships in general. Getting away from social media and instead focusing on sociability in your home and in your activities goes a long way toward fostering a long-term sense of well-being. Human beings are social animals, after all, and working to improve those social relationships is certainly part of the recipe for achieving lasting happiness.

Achieving happiness through hygge involves focusing on creating a cozy space and a comforting lifestyle; this facilitates and nurtures happier feelings. For example, if your home is a space of refuge - a calm, shared space with a warm fire, decorated with soothing natural materials - then you are likely to feel protected, safe, and calm. We will explore more about how to create this kind of ideal space in Chapter 4.

The application of hygge in your life boils down to a few key features, all of which will be discussed at greater length in the following chapters. These are crucial elements to letting hygge into your life: warm lighting, such as candlelight, is perhaps the most important element in igniting the hygge spirit in your home. Texture in clothing (or anything touching your skin) is also important, as all things soft and warm are key to promoting a calm and relaxed environment. Think cozy socks or a soft throw. The décor in your home also plays a role in promoting hygge, with the use of natural elements taking precedence over the cold, hard surfaces of glass and steel. This also applies to the use of color: neutral, warm colors are more inviting than bold, overwhelming ones. Beige and cream, with light hints of color, is more calming than bright reds, yellows, or oranges. Obviously, hygge - coming from a cold, northern clime - is also all about warmth, but not just regarding room temperature. Internal, psychological warmth is a result of providing a safe and comfortable environment for everyone who enters your space -

yourself included. An inviting space is a harmonious space. Also, think about how you arrange your space: togetherness is a key component of hygge, and people within that space should feel connected and comforted by each other as well as their environment.

Activities suggested by the hygge lifestyle all reflect tenants described above. This is not about hosting formal dinners or leading loud rounds of competitive games. It could be anything from simple conversation to a home-style dinner to coffee and cards at the end of an evening. Whatever you plan in your space, attune it to the goal of togetherness and connection with your family and friends.

Last, don't limit yourself to practicing hygge just in your home or on your days off. This is a lifestyle that takes time to cultivate, carrying with it the worthwhile goal of improving your happiness, health, and well-being. Implement some of these strategies at your place of employment when possible and appropriate. Reflect on the benefits of walking into an office with soft lighting, personal and pleasant pictures, with perhaps a plant or two. That office is infinitely more inviting than one with harsh overhead lights and nothing more personal than a desktop computer. Think about a mental health professional's office; most are purposefully designed to comfort and soothe the patients who enter there. This can also be your purpose at work, putting clients or others at ease as well as lowering your own levels of stress.

Think about other ways to cultivate the hygge spirit throughout your daily activities. Communing with nature, rather than zoning out with our technological devices, is one sure way to practice the habit of hygge. Take a leisurely bike ride and walk along the trails to experience the natural world; be present and unhurried in how you approach activity. The goal is to feel calm and peaceful, not frantic and competitive. Slow down a bit: the contemporary American lifestyle is geared to go at lightning speed, and this often means we miss out on the little joys, such as listening to birdsong or watching a sunset. You can also think of hygge as a way to do good in the world, albeit in small, incremental ways. Practice sustainability for the greater common good. Recycling, eating locally produced foods, and seeking out environmentally friendly power sources are all activities that adhere to the overall spirit of hygge.

You can also carry hygge with you throughout your day via your attitude, your way of presenting yourself, your way of connecting with others - even strangers. In the next chapter, we will explore the many little things that can make up our peaceful day while practicing hygge.

Chapter 3: Practical Hygge: How to Have a Danish Day

While most Americans begin and end their days in a dead run:

> gulping coffee and -if you're lucky – breakfast
> getting the kids to school
> dodging traffic
> making it to work on time
> catching up on emails
> work-work-work
> getting kids to activities
> rushing home
> eating take-out or leftovers on the go
> collapsing into bed

This clearly the opposite of how to have a Danish day! The emphasis is not on accomplishing tasks or ticking off items on a list; the emphasis is on living a present and happy life. Instead of focusing on instant gratification or realizing consumerist fantasies, the Danes seek to experience relationships with people and their environment.

Let's imagine how we might immerse ourselves in a Danish day of hygge: simple, practical, interactive, *and happy.*

Good Morning!

After a wonderfully well-rested night, you wake up to light the candles around the house, giving off a soft, warm glow that brings you gently into the day. The house is neat and simple, organized but comfortable, with just enough of what you need without the clutter of conspicuous consumption. Make a generous cup of cocoa - or rich, dark coffee - and have a slice of dense, comforting rugbrød (Danish rye bread). Or, perhaps a big bowl of porridge is more appropriate to fuel your day, complete with whole grains, some sliced fruit and a handful of chopped nuts sprinkled over it all. If it's a weekday, get ready to go to your workspace for five or six hours. Greet your colleagues warmly - for they are friends - and finish your work without fear of missing out on home life, because you will be seeing your family this evening.

If you are Danish, you are most likely working in a position that affords you a solid and stable life. Remember, a Dane's post-high school education is free, leading to a workplace that is less competitive and more collaborative. Remember that work should be a place that fulfills your need to be creative. We should all be productive, contributing to the world around us, and because we are only concerned with amassing money or status! In Denmark, the gap between the wealthy and the not-so-wealthy is the lowest in the world; everyone has the chance to live a secure and contented life. If you were to lose your job, then the government would help you out - up to 90 percent of your paycheck would be provided for about four years as a cushion until you found another opportunity. Work is satisfying because it is a career of choice, and your workspace is nearly as inviting as your home. It doesn't feel like drudgery because it is not the only important thing in your life, as your supervisor and your colleagues well know! Work is one part of a full life, and you do not take it home with you. Instead, you leave in the afternoon, ready to enjoy the rest of what life has to offer.

Good Afternoon

It is afternoon, and that is the perfect time to spend some of it outdoors. At home, you have large windows that allow you to bask in the sunlight during the long summer days or revel in the snow and storms that carry on during the short winter days. Each day, you plan to spend some time outside in the fresh air, communing with nature. Perhaps you decide to go to the park, where you will invariably run into someone you know, a friend perhaps or a neighbor. Maybe you will meet them there for an afternoon picnic if the weather cooperates. No matter: Danish weather is always unpredictable, but you are always prepared. A picnic in the park could just as easily become an afternoon spent in a café. You'll probably spend time with friends in the café in any case. It's the Danish thing to do!

You hop on your bike - nine out of ten Danes have one, often using them daily - getting exercise that doesn't feel like exercise while you amble over to the café. You've already had your simple lunch - some smørrebrød of liver pâté, herring or roast pork. Now, the café is time for a nice cup of coffee or cocoa and, of course, a lovely sweet, perhaps a pastry or a big slice of cake. Fulfilling sweets are definitely a part of practical hygge - all that walking and biking and communing with nature gives you more reason to indulge. You meet with some friends, a nice intimate group of three or four where you can talk about your work, the weather, the kids, whatever strikes your fancy. The important part of each day is socializing and being together with your friends. One of your friends brings her newborn in a stroller, and since the weather is nice, you all sit outside while you share thoughts and coffee and cake. Your friend is enjoying her generous maternity leave; she gets a very fulfilling full year to spend with her child before she returns to work. Everyone shares in this humane opportunity to nurture a newborn, a perk of the Danish social welfare system.

Once you have finished your leisurely café break, it is off to the market, where you go to purchase some fresh produce and other ingredients for the evening meal. This is a significant part of the day, something that you do most days because cooking and eating together is a very important part of daily life. In addition, the practice of hygge emphasizes fostering local relationships and contributing to the good in the world: shopping at the market is an excellent way to fulfill all these elements. You build relationships with the farmers, the proprietors, and you buy the healthiest and freshest food that you can find to nurture yourself and your family. It's not about fancy and fussy ingredients, but rather fresh and wholesome ones for the simple meal that you will prepare - with the help of your partner or family or friends - for supper that night.

When you get home from your forays, you decide to take a little time for self-care. Perhaps you light some candles in the bathroom and take a soothing bath before preparing the evening meal. If it's summer, perhaps you sit outside with another cup of coffee and enjoy the afternoon sunlight with the paper or a puzzle, or you simply spend some time relaxing with your own thoughts. Go ahead; this is what the hyggelige is all about. It takes some re-charging to re-energize! If it's winter, perhaps you make a fire and wrap yourself in a blanket in your cozy hyggekrog (hygge corner) and pick up a good book to read. Whatever you decide, it is never a bad idea to spend some time in self-care, treating yourself to some calming moments of your own choosing. Once you are re-charged, you'll be ready and eager for some family and friend time.

Good Evening

Now you are ready to begin preparing the evening meal. The family is all at home by now - everyone knows that the evening meal is to be spent together and that friends are always welcome - and everyone of age contributes to the preparation and presentation of the meal. Because this is a typical Danish day, you have decided to make something hearty and healthy, simple but full of comforting flavor. Perhaps you have decided to make stegtflaesk, one of the national dishes of the Danes, consisting of some crispy pork and boiled potatoes with parsley-cream sauce. Or, perhaps you are just channeling the spirit of hygge and decide to make an earthy stew with some meat and vegetables that you bought at the market - something simple that requires just a bit of time to prepare, then a nice while to cook whilst filling the house with comforting aromas. This gives you time to talk with family and friends, make a warming drink or two, and set the table so that everyone feels welcome and comfortable. Certainly, setting the atmosphere is one of the key aspects of hygge, and you like to present a table with some nice tableware and/or flowers and/or decorative vases. The focus is not about the objects themselves, but rather about making the table an inviting and pleasant place to want to gather around. Of course, everyone has turned off their phones and set aside their tablets or laptops, because this is all about spending quality time together.

Once dinner is ready, everyone gathers and eats, family-style, relishing the simple pleasures of dining together on good, fresh food that is prepared in the home and eaten as a family. This may be one of the most crucial pieces to the puzzle of Danish happiness: this kind of special family time isn't saved for special occasions at all. These times are everyday events, fostering a culture of kindness, generosity, and gratitude. One could even suggest that the high rates of happiness and low rates of poverty and crime are borne of the simple fact that breaking bread together is one of the most powerful unifiers within any society. Some would say that once that is lost, there is a kind of fellowship that is sorely missed. Hence, the Danish emphasis on work-life balance is so deeply ingrained in the culture. Danes feel that you are not truly living without having this unifying time spent with loved ones, fostering meaningful relationships, and sharing your life with others.

After dinner, as darkness falls - in summer, this will be late; in winter, dusk comes quite early - you gather in your cozy space, with intimate room for all. Perhaps you decide to play some friendly games together, or it is time for casual conversation. If you and your partner or spouse are on your own, you may decide to watch a film together, snuggled in a warm blanket in front of a fire or bathed in candlelight. Perhaps you are on your own for the evening, which gives you the chance to return to your hyggekrog and spend a glorious couple of hours reading a wonderful book. Because your day has been spent enjoying each moment without stress and hurry or the feeling that you never have time to accomplish enough, you fall asleep easily and dream lightly of another beautiful hyggelige day.

The Takeaway

Hygge itself is nearly undefinable in English: for some, it indicates a lifestyle, as loosely outlined above; for others, it indicates a personal feeling of cozy comfort. For others, it indicates a mindset of being present in each moment of the day. Basically, the combination of all three will get you closest to the experience of hygge in a typical Danish day. The reason for hygge's recent popularity seems to need little explanation: in a harried world of stress and demands, hygge represents a return to something that is simpler, happier, and ultimately more fulfilling.

Certainly, Danish society is set up for hygge, with its generous welfare state, equal and stable wages, and a cultural penchant for work-life balance. Not only do Danes have the shortest workweek in Europe (around 35 hours for most), but they also are afforded at least five weeks of paid vacation a year, and mothers have paid maternity leave for a full year. There are also social safety nets of all kinds, from free education through university to unemployment benefits that pay up to 90 percent of your salary for up to four years. Extreme poverty and homelessness are virtually unknown throughout Denmark, and health care is nationalized and free. All of this comes at the cost of taxpayers, of course, and Danes pay the highest tax rates of just about any country in the world (close to 60 percent in 2019). Still, most Danes do not complain about the high tax rate because of the social benefits that everyone receives. It is a rare instance of a truly egalitarian society wherein most people believe that their country will be better off if everyone were educated, healthy, and taken care of when necessary.

When we look around at other Western countries, particularly America, we see a vast gap between the very wealthy and the very poor, something which doesn't exist in Denmark. The trade-off, as some would argue, is that you don't really have the opportunity to get rich in Denmark; everyone is educated, salaries are comparable across the board. Elevating your own status is not easily done. A typical Danish response might be to suggest that happiness does not equate with wealth or status. Danes have little to fear from crime or other ills that societies with great wealth inequality face. These are just a few societal norms that give Danes little reason to change their present system.

If you are a woman in Danish society, then you might even have a more beneficial view of this system. For many reasons, Danish women do not feel pressure to get married. Their society is so egalitarian; women have as much education and opportunity as men. They have access to the same kinds of stable, well-paying jobs. Women do not have to rely on men for money or status. Second, with the generous maternity leave and unemployment benefits, women can achieve a much greater balance between work and life, especially regarding having and raising a family. This is one of the most important aspects of Danish culture that other Western countries would do well to consider. Third, shifting the emphasis away from marriage as a transactional relationship means that it can become a more emotionally satisfying one; you can focus on fostering a relationship rather than achieving a contractual marriage.

So, Danish societal systems are set up in line with the practice of hygge! Living elsewhere, many do not necessarily enjoy the benefits and security of that particular national way of life. If the hygge way of life appears to you, it is still possible to introduce elements of hygge into your daily routine with thoughtfulness and care. Who isn't drawn to a life of less stress, more mindfulness, and cozy contentment? This is what starting to practice hygge requires: a desire to create an atmosphere conducive to comfort and calm, a focus on togetherness and family rather than work and status, and a belief that material wealth and consumer products do not equal happiness. Rather, it is an intrinsic feeling that comes from leading a comforting life of self-care and well-being. There are many ways to achieve this mindset and practice this lifestyle, and the following chapters will give you many specific ideas of how to introduce this Danish experience into your life.

The Checklist

Self-care is the key! Hygge is about giving yourself permission to set down all your stresses and worries and making sure that you are healthy and happy - only then can you help others be happy and healthy, as well.

Atmosphere cements the mindset. Soft lighting - most Danes agree that without candlelight, there can be no hyggelige. It is a must - along with earthy and comforting décor, big windows when possible, simplicity of design and a minimum of clutter. Less stuff equals more life.

Simplicity, simplicity, simplicity! Hygge is all about appreciating the simple pleasures in life: get outdoors, talk with friends, spend time in a café, read a good book, stay in the present, and appreciate what you have.

Speaking of the outdoors, get out there every day. Fresh air and wholesome exercise – riding a bike or playing in the park - are also crucial to cultivating the practice of hygge. Nature should be an inspiration to enjoy daily.

Café culture is important all over Europe, but it is certainly a huge part of the hygge lifestyle. This is about being with friends, enjoying warming drinks and tasty (read: sugary) foods. Cafés are central to the Danish day.

Markets are also significant. Kitchens are small and spare in much of Europe in general, and daily shopping at the local market is a way of life for many. It's a way to commune with others, to contribute to the community, and to provide healthy local food and goods for your family.

Prepare dinner at home and eat together - *every day* – or at least as often as is practically possible. Turn off phones and other devices and make each evening a gathering that's worthy of a holiday season.

Success is not defined via one material thing. Rather, success is about work-life balance, creativity, and productivity in your life, comfort, and happiness in your home.

Chapter 4: Practical Hygge: Hygge Your House

If you've ever encountered Old Norse mythology or traditional Scandinavian poetry, you will encounter one overarching theme: the absolute inviolable importance of the security and sanctity of home and hearth. In *Beowulf*, a famous old tale involving Danes and Swedes and probably the most famous embraced by English-speakers, our hero must combat the ravages that the beast Grendel has perpetrated on the great hall of Heorot. Grendel's sin is to flout the unbreakable conventions of hospitality and to violate the safe haven that is the home and hearth of King Hrothgar's great peoples.

This social law of hospitality runs deep within Scandinavian culture, the remnant of a time when harsh winters and poor harvests could leave people homeless and starving. You are never to turn a stranger away, and you welcome all with the greatest of hospitality, no matter how humble your offerings.

While hygge itself is a more recent - and perhaps more modulated - take on the importance of home and hearth, the general rules of hospitality apply. It is linked to a long and lasting tradition in which the most important social interactions take place in a warm and safe environment wherein food and drink - and stories - are shared. Out of this, modern Danes have embraced hygge, with its emphasis on simple pleasures and café culture, the togetherness of people, and the fostering of happiness on self-care and social interaction – not material goods.

Not only is hygge a state of mind wherein you create a feeling of well-being and comfort, but it also encompasses a particular visual style and atmospheric component that assists in the overall feeling of contentment. In recent years, designers and other influencers have promoted the Danish look in home décor and in entertainment venues, and this is easy to replicate in your home. "Hygge-fying" your house is important if you truly want to change your lifestyle, as your home is your primary place of experience. There are many ways in which you can personalize your hygge home, of course, but the following are some guidelines for the elements that are most important in unlocking a hygge-inspired sense of comfort and happiness.

Whole House Hygge

There are certain elements of hygge style that are relevant and welcome in any space in the home. Some of these elements have to do with creating an overall atmosphere of welcome, warmth, comfort, and coziness, while others are about creating a look that supports the atmosphere you are trying to achieve. It cannot be overstated how important it is to "hygge your house up" if you want to live a hygge life; the comfort and centrality of home and hearth is one of the central tenants in this Danish philosophy.

> **Lighting**: this is one of the most crucial elements to creating a hygge atmosphere in your home. As mentioned in the beginning chapters, most Danes see a direct link between candles and hygge - indeed; many say that, without candles, there can be no hygge home spirit. Thus, what many Americans might see as a fire hazard is essential to this way of life in Denmark. Just exercise common sense and a dose of

caution when placing and lighting candles throughout your home, and you should have no problems. Aside from candles, think about accent lighting - small lamps in corners of rooms; dimmer switches for larger spaces - rather than harsh, overhead lighting. Natural light is also warm and inviting, depending on the time of year and angle of the sun; in hygge homes, windows are generally large and uncovered to allow for the natural world to glow within the home. As we all know from dining out or snuggling up with a date on the couch, lighting is key to setting a mood; the mood that you want to set in your hygge home is one of soothing comfort. Soft lighting should be the rule of the day throughout the home.

Other visual elements: color is also important to the hygge home, with an emphasis on neutral, serene colors that serve to complement the soft, natural lighting and contribute to the soothing sensibility of the home. Look out for too much embellishment, which distracts from the overall effect of coziness.

Music: almost as crucial as lighting in terms of setting a mood, what we listen to often impacts how we feel about the world around us. This might mean that in your hygge home, silence is best in order to allow the sounds of nature to carry through if you live in a rural area or are vacationing in a cabin in the woods). If you live in a bustling city or a crowded building, setting mood music throughout the home is an excellent way to enhance the hygge atmosphere. Again, the emphasis is on soothing comfort, rather than rousing loudness; perhaps classical music fits your style, or soft jazz, or simple instrumentals. Check the volume, too; this should be background music, not a distraction from the conversation and activities with family and friends.

Warmth: this is also a key element within a hygge home, which makes perfect sense if you come from a northern clime. Denmark has famously cold and long winters, so hygge must have been developed, in part, to deal with this kind of climactic onslaught. It's also psychologically potent, the idea of refuge in the middle of the storm, that all of us can relate to no matter where we come from. A haven in the middle of tumultuous weather is a trope that we encounter in literature as far back as Homer and his *Odyssey*. Aside from that, the idea of welcome is emphasized by warmth. For these reasons, be sure to check temperatures throughout your home, seeing to it that everyone who visits feels warm (shorthand for welcomed and secure). Also, think of providing blankets - not just on beds but also around the home - as a kind of useable décor, providing warmth and comfort wherever a person may choose to wander.

Create Hyggekrogs: there should be a comfortable and cozy nook in every home, and ideally, your hygge home will have more than one or two. A cushion and blanket in front of the fireplace, a window seat in the bedroom, a divan in the office for reading, or a sunroom with a rocking chair. These are all quiet places where you, your family, or your friends can curl up with a good book or a journal or a simple mug of coffee and your own thoughts. These little nooks should be cozied-up with blankets, cushions, and soft lighting to accommodate anyone's daily self-care.

Nice Smells: anyone who remembers visits to their grandparents' home might well remember the cozy smell of baking bread or cookies or pie. If you are lucky, these scents remind you of your own home growing up. If a home is lit beautifully and decorated with care, it matters little if it doesn't also have a lovely smell to go with it. As anyone who has read Proust knows, scent triggers our strongest memories, and this atmospheric element should not be forgotten. Short of baking bread or pastries, you could arrange flowers or plants throughout the house, making sure that they aren't overpowering or allergy-causing. There are many natural scents available to add an alluring touch to space. Again, the key here is subtlety; too much scent is an irritation, and too many competing scents become a distraction.

Natural Décor: when choosing your décor for your hygge home, focus on using natural elements such as wood, dried flowers, stone, and other items straight from nature. One of the emphases within hygge living is to respect and enjoy nature, so using natural elements in your décor keeps within that tenant. This is also an excellent way to practice another Danish habit: recycling. Danes are frugal in the sense that it is frowned upon to let anything go to waste, so re-using old bits and pieces of natural materials is certainly within the hygge spirit. This is also in the spirit of de-emphasizing consumer culture, as many elements of Danish décor could easily be "found" items: pebbles from the local lake fill a jar on the sideboard table; flowers from the field behind the house are dried to fill a vase at the table; seeds and beans are layered in mason jars to display in the kitchen. Embrace what is imperfect and look at old objects in a different way; there is much beauty to be found in trinkets and keepsakes you already have in your possession. Use your imagination and your location to determine how to put together your own personalized hygge home. Think about the color scheme, as well, using natural and neutral colors rather than bright, overbearing ones.

Texture in Décor: another consideration when adding items to beautify your hygge home is to add layers of texture. The most important texture in the hygge spirit is that of softness - warm socks, cozy blankets, smooth sheets - but when layered with a bit of variety, texture can dress up the minimalist Danish look in clean and subtle ways. Again, stick to natural elements when thinking of texture, such as leather and wool or woods of different grains; use a healthy dose of restraint, as a hygge home is a minimalist home.

Neatness: another key to creating a hygge home that is welcoming to all is to keep it neat and tidy; clutter detracts from the soothing atmosphere that you've worked so hard to achieve, as well as takes away from your focus on living life rather than accumulating stuff. A hygge home is by no means an austere home, with sharp edges and sparse spaces. It is, in fact, quite the opposite, with inviting blankets and comforting corners in which to curl up. It is also clean and neat without extraneous material to interrupt the interactions among others or your calming rituals of self-care.

Living Area

The most important thing to remember about your living area is that it is the heart of the home (alongside the kitchen), and there is a reason why the terms "home and hearth" go together: most ideal hygge homes will have a fireplace. It provides warmth and soft lighting, as well as a reminder of nature within the home itself. But do not despair if you live in a hearth-less home: make your own. It is undoubtedly cheating to put on a virtual image of a flickering fire on the television set. However, if this is an option, it shouldn't be dismissed. Even a virtual fire can help to create an atmosphere of warmth. Seeing and hearing a fire creates a Pavlovian response in most, triggering sensations of warmth and comfort regardless of the fire's reality. Certainly, gas log fireplaces create that illusion. Fire is also quite symbolic across all cultures, representing warmth and symbolizing fellowship, food, the cooking of meat, and breaking of bread. It brings both light and life, and a fire glows with the possibility of shelter and comfort at the end of a long journey. Hospitality is embedded in the idea of the hearth, and fire's romantic association with our past selves and historical cultures are not soon forgotten. While the fire itself is simply a source of warmth and light, its actual atmospheric importance far outweighs its practical usage.

Create a central focal point of the room wherein everyone can gather around comfortably (the basic idea of a hearth) such as a low coffee table surrounded by cushions and blankets to sit on, or a scattering of comfy chairs that are set up to invite conversation. Most of us automatically make our television set/entertainment center the focal point of our living area; while there is nothing inherently wrong with this, it isn't the best way to set up a space for interaction and togetherness. If that's how your living area is arranged, consider setting up a secondary hearth area for those hyggelige times, such as when the electronics are silent, and the guests are interacting.

Bedrooms

Obviously, guest bedrooms should be as warm and inviting as your own. In fact, many home experts will suggest you spend a night or two in your own guest bedroom to see what creature comforts are missing before subjecting your friends or family to it! Clearly, the beds should be warm with plenty of blankets, and everything should be tidy with space enough to accommodate guests.

Some other small things to think about that can make all the difference in a hygge home: have some books available for anyone to read, choosing topics with comfort and security in mind, as well as age appropriateness. Put out a small bowl or dish with non-perishable snacks in them so that a guest can help herself to a midnight snack if she likes. Decorate with some fairy lights if candles aren't a feasible option. Put out a couple of personal keepsakes as decoration, rather than something without emotional charge. Again, think of what you want to have at hand when you spend quality time in your bedroom during an afternoon or overnight. Your guest should want to stay in bed an extra hour or two, just for the sheer pleasure or relaxation.

Bathrooms

One of the undeniable facts about bathrooms is that they tend to accumulate clutter quickly. They contain items we use every day, and it becomes the path of least resistance to leaving everything lying about. In a hygge home, you should consider two things to complement the whole home atmosphere you've worked hard to set up. First, find a reasonable place to put away everything that you use daily, and then – if you don't have a space for everything, *consider minimizing your bathroom clutter*. Since one of the points of hygge is appreciating simplicity, perhaps you don't need four different kinds of shampoo, or ten different shades of eye shadow. This is part of the mindset of living a simple, present life.

In terms of a guest bathroom, think comfort: warm, soft towels with extras just in case, a drawer or cabinet with common toiletry items for guests to use when needed, some bath products and comfy robes to encourage a soothing soak. Think of your bathroom as a minimalist spa area - you get the idea.

Kitchen and Dining

Besides the living area, the kitchen area is the most central part of the home, where you bring people together, providing nourishment and love. In addition to simple, hearty food, always have some warming drinks on hand, coffee and tea and cocoa for sure. Kitchen lighting can often be harsh - strong lighting is necessary for accurate cooking – so be sure to consider other light sources for when everyone gathers in the kitchen. Set out bowls of fruit as décor and/or a snack and be sure to keep the kitchen tidy like the rest of the house - it's impossible to cook well in a disorganized kitchen.

When dining, set the table. It doesn't matter if your placemats, tablecloths, dishes, or glasses are expensive and fancy; it matters that you are creating an atmosphere. Paper plates and plastic cups just don't scream warm and inviting, and self-service at the table is far more attractive and interactive than grabbing a plate and loading it up yourself before wandering into the living room to eat in front of the television. Two rules of thumb in my own household is that dinner is never eaten with the television on or devices in hand, and the table is always set - however humbly - with individual place settings and platters and bowls set out for everyone to help themselves family style. For many, this may sound like extra work, but if you practice hygge with the right spirit, it is another way to build community and relationships around the table, as well as encouraging everyone to contribute.

Outside the Home

Even though this next depends in part on where you live, creating a hygge home also entails having an outdoor space for gathering and interacting. This can be a back porch with a comfortable set of chairs arranged around a portable hearth or firepit. It can be a balcony with some lovely plants and a view. It could be a garden equipped with a gazebo or a central picnic area. It could even be a driveway, some foldout chairs, and a good sunset. Whatever your situation, the hygge home should have some sort of outdoor component, weather permitting. An improvised picnic in the backyard is just as hyggelige as warming your hands around a campfire.

The Checklist

The atmosphere is everything, and lighting is perhaps the most crucial aspect of creating the right hygge atmosphere. Candles are key, but there are many other ways to provide soft, natural-looking light, as well.

Keep it pure and simple: hygge is about minimalist comfort, not clutter and consumption.

Think about a hearth, whether it be a roaring fire, a virtual one, or an improvised focal point to your living area. There should be a comfortable gathering place in which good conversation and good company are fostered.

Décor should complement the hygge atmosphere rather than detract; think of found materials, natural elements, and neutral colors for the best results.

Think of all five senses when creating your hygge home: sight (lighting, color scheme, tidiness), sound (soft music or natural noise), smell (baking bread, dried flowers, other natural scents), touch (soft blankets, natural textures), and taste (warming drinks, simple and hearty food, sweet snacks).

Think of every room in your house as a sanctuary of sorts, a calm and comforting refuge that encourages both independent self-care and communal togetherness.

Chapter 5: Practical Hygge: How to Hygge Your Wardrobe

Hygge is not just for your home or your holiday, it is also for your everyday living. According to some of the foremost experts on hygge (namely, Meik Wiking, as mentioned in Chapter 1), just about everything you do and own can be "hygge'd." Thus, fashion trends have also caught up with the explosion of popularity regarding this Danish lifestyle, and if you want to look - and feel - the part, designers and outlets have more than enough to offer. Likewise, making your wardrobe more hygge in spirit need not cost a fortune, as the keyword is comfort - you probably have some hyggelige items in your closet right now.

Keeping in line with all the aforementioned information regarding hygge style, your hygge'd wardrobe would consist of neutral colors, some insist on lots of black, and soft textures, with scarfs and cozy socks galore. The layering of clothes is also in the hygge spirit, and this makes sense as the trend is coming from a chilly winter climate.

Why hygge your wardrobe? To help yourself feel an overall sense of well-being, to feel that your lifestyle is embracing you in a warming hug, you need to feel warm and comfortable in all your clothes. Learning to relax and stay in the present moment during your daily life requires clothes that aren't fussy, that can be stylish without being uncomfortable, that can be minimalist yet fashion-forward. As with any wardrobe, there are excellent hygge styles for the range of what you do, from going out to a café to biking or cavorting in the park to staying in for dinner with the family. Anything in the hygge style will be relaxed and comfortable, and the fact that the fashion world has caught wind of this trend means that some of it can be quite beautiful in an understated manner.

Basically, you want your clothing to match your mood. Just as your home décor sets an atmosphere conducive to the stress-free happiness of hygge, so can your wardrobe set the stage for a feeling of hygge that goes with you everywhere.

The Checklist

Knitwear is essential to the hygge style. Not only is it comfortable and affordable, but it is also easy to take care of - no special care instructions, for the most part. Soft and flowing lines define the style.

Oversize separates are also very much in keeping with the trend of hygge, especially oversize sweaters. This is a style that never really goes out of fashion, in any case - at least around the house. For going out, a neutrally colored cardigan is the perfect accessory to round out an outfit *and* to keep you warm throughout the day.

Socks, socks, and more socks: one of the primary components of any hygge wardrobe is an ample supply of cozy, comfy socks - bulky for wearing around the house, especially when you're curled up in your hyggekrog reading a book, and sleeker socks for treks to the café to fit into your favorite pair of loafers.

Athletic leisurewear has dominated the fashion industry for years now; the hygge twist on that is fleece wear. A bit looser and softer, fleece pants free you from the stiffness of denim and can be dressed up or down, depending on the occasion. Try a comfortable blazer to dress them up or stick to an oversized sweater or cardigan for more casual wear.

Aside from comfy socks, the most signature hygge fashion item is the scarf. Like the oversized sweater, the scarf comes in an almost endless variety of shapes and sizes, from big and bulky a la Harry Potter, or sleek and skinny. Whatever your preference, keep in mind that the scarf is not only a fashion accessory but a necessary piece of clothing in colder climates: scarfs should be both practical and pretty to fit the hygge spirit.

Also, don't ditch the sweater - or even the scarf - during the warmer months of spring or early fall. Instead, look for less bulky and/or less lengthy sweaters and sleek scarfs of lightweight material to accentuate your look any time of the year. The function of these is to give you a feeling of comfortable security, even if you don't absolutely need them for the practical purpose of warmth.

Layering your look is also very hyggelige. Like the oversized sweater and the bulky scarf, layering can serve a very practical purpose and is also in keeping with the free spirit that underlies the hygge philosophy. In addition, this is another nod to the actual climate out of which hygge grows: the weather in Denmark is notoriously changeable, so layering is an excellent way to be prepared for whatever the weather happens to throw your way. It may be gloomy on your way to the office, but sunny and warmer by the time you bike over to meet your friends at the local café, or vice versa. As one famous Danish saying goes, "In Denmark, there is no bad weather, only bad clothes." Layering prepares you for any kind of weather and allows you to enjoy your day - no matter what the heavens dictate.

Robes for wear around the house are absolutely hyggelige, as well. Keeping a robe handy for whatever season is an excellent way to invite self-care and moderate indulgence. Stepping into a comfy robe out of the shower in the morning practically begs you to brew another mug of coffee or cocoa and sit in your cozy nook with a book or a crafting project.

Invest in at least a couple, one for warmer months and one for colder.

As mentioned above, neutral colors are more in tune with the hygge spirit than bold or bright colors and patterns. Pale hues like beiges and whites are certainly hygge, though black is another popular choice. Muted black -like charcoal - are very much a part of hygge fashion. Wearing all black - especially in slightly varying shades - is quite chic without being severe if it's done with hygge in mind (that is, loose, flowing, and layered).

An actual Danish fashion import is also a must-have for fashionable acolytes of hygge: the style of the sweater worn by Sarah Lund, the main character in the immensely popular television series, *The Killing*. It can be described as an ever-so-slightly oversized knit sweater with a bit of an understated pattern on it. This is the perfect sweater for an afternoon outing during cooler months.

Remember: even if you are going out for a more formal evening, it is possible to capture the spirit of hygge: stay warm, above all else. Don't be afraid to layer a long comfortable cardigan or woolen jacket with a fancy dress for eveningwear. If there's one thing hygge doesn't support, it's feeling cold - quite the opposite of well-being or the warmth of a hug.

In terms of your hygge wardrobe, it is primarily, a wardrobe centered around the same feeling of staying in a cozy, warm, and comfortable house. Thus, most of your hygge wardrobe doesn't have to be fancy or new or impressive. If you were to think in highly fashionable terms, you could think about coordinating your wardrobe with your interior design - both practical and in keeping with the hygge spirit. Either way, you undoubtedly have a handful of comfortable sweaters, cardigans, and fleece pants for your everyday home wear already; utilize those and invest in a few nicer items for meeting friends or going out to dinner. Now you have a personal hygge style to take with you anywhere!

You can also think about hygge beyond your wardrobe into your beauty regimen itself. The hygge style is pure and simple, and this is exactly what your skincare and makeup regime should also be. A neutral color palette, excellent moisturizers, and maybe some essential oils and exfoliant are all you need to maintain a lovely glow that comes from both within – practicing the happiness of hygge – and from without.

In the spirit of hygge, celebrate the little joys in life and stay present in every moment: this shouldn't require you to overthink your daily attire, or to feel obligated to dress for someone else's ideals. Self-care means respecting the self, just as you take the time to nurture your physical health. In this way, a hygge wardrobe celebrates a woman's desire to look pretty without submitting herself to the whims of the others: other women, men, or fashion magazines. This does not mean that dressing in hygge style is not attractive or sexy! Hygge dress attire is simply designed by women for a woman's needs. It's pretty and practical, comfortable and cozy - an excellent way to present yourself as a working woman, as a woman of means, as a mother, as a friend. It should express your personal style and savvy.

A hygge mindset is also about slowing down and reducing excess. Your wardrobe can – and should – express that; coordinating an inordinate number of fussy accessories isn't in the spirit of enjoying your daily life without encumbrance. Practical considerations should drive the choice of accessories rather than any top-down kind of fashionista thinking. This puts you in the driver's seat, prompting you to become an active consumer rather than a passive purchaser. Again, practical can be pretty - sometimes even prettier than artifice. So, when considering your hygge lifestyle, remember to let your natural beauty shine through – even through your choice of attire.

Hygge is also about relaxation, avoiding the daily grind that often drives people to succumb to pressures and external demands rather than internal joys and practical pleasures. It is difficult to feel relaxed in clothing that is restrictive or *so bright and bold* that all eyes are on you all the time. Instead of working so diligently to impress others, we should be working hard to help ourselves to happiness and serenity. One way to turn down the pressures of everyday life is to allow yourself to wear clothing that is comfortable and free, that reminds you of how to maintain a sense of calm security.

Ultimately, hygge - especially for working women, torn between so many conflicting demands - is about being kinder to yourself. Giving yourself the time, space, and permission to relax and to enjoy the simple pleasures in life is one of the greatest gifts you can give yourself. In this current era of constant self-improvement, we are told that we must work harder and harder to get healthier and better. This fallacy often reads as one simple thing, especially for women: thinner. While there is a contemporary rage for all things authentic (from food to craft beer to old-world artisanal products to repurposed furniture and handmade pickles), this new vogue tends to skip over women in terms of how they are asked to present themselves. Supermodels and movie stars dominate the pages of glossy magazines, movie screens, and our televisions; for most, this idea of beauty is both unattainable and unhealthy. This is where the influence of hygge is slowly-but-surely being felt. Over the past couple of decades, changes in social attitudes, and the rapid growth of technology have allowed us to see many kinds of people in all shapes, sizes, and profiles of beauty. Hygge is one trend that has embraced the idea that beauty isn't simply one ideal, and it shouldn't be difficult or uncomfortable. Indeed, it should be easy, cozy, comfortable, and uniquely *you*. This philosophy has been a driving force behind Danish culture for many years, and it has led to one of the most female-friendly cultures in the world - not to mention giving birth to the happiest people on earth! Hygge is not merely a passing trend, but a true way of life that could teach us all a little about self-love and kindness.

Chapter 6: Practical Hygge: Hungry for Hygge

As with any long-standing tradition in any culture across the world, food plays a significant role. It would be difficult to think of Thanksgiving without turkey, for example, or to imagine St. Patrick's Day without soda bread and beer. Aside from these secular examples, cultures with deep-seated religious traditions also have accompanying foods, such as matzo during Passover or dates to break the daily fast during Ramadan. Denmark is overwhelmingly Christian in its religious traditions, and we will discuss how hygge and holidays - Christmas and Easter, for example - work together in the next chapter. Hygge itself is an entrenched secular tradition in Danish culture, and it also gives rise to particular kinds of foods and drinks that have a specific spirit of well-being and comfort.

What makes a food hyggelige? Warm and welcoming comfort foods fit the category to a tee: just as the word hygge can be etymologically traced back to "hug," the foods you eat while practicing hygge should represent a hug from the inside-out. Since hygge is also about communion between family and friends, hyggelige food is meant to be shared with loved ones at the table – with plenty of conversation and interaction. This can be in a café, having some fika (snacks to be consumed with warm drinks), or it can be in your own home, enjoying a home-cooked dinner. Hygge isn't directly concerned with health - a sugar bun is very hygge while celery sticks are decidedly not - but it does encourage moderation. The hygge emphasis on outdoor activity certainly balances the significant cocoa and cake consumption, or at least that is the idea! Eating hyggelige isn't about guilt or self-restraint; it is about health in the sense of self-care, comfort, and communion with others. Breaking bread with others has always been a sacrosanct act, and hygge emphasizes the joys and pleasures of sharing food around a crowded table.

Buns and Bread for Breakfast

As hearsay would have it, breakfast is the most important meal of the day, and that couldn't be truer when starting your hyggelige day. A large, steaming mug of coffee or cocoa (or tea, if one prefers) is a must to get you going on a chilly morning, accompanied by a hearty breakfast to fuel you on your bike ride, for your daily work, or simply to encourage you to get a fire going before you settle into your cozy nook with a good book. The following recipes are just a quick representation of all that Danish food has to offer for breaking the fast each morning. Remember: hygge food doesn't have to be exclusively Danish! A freshly baked biscuit with some sausage gravy or a plate of warm waffles stuffed with either pecans or bacon and covered in syrup would also fit the bill quite nicely. Try these ideas below for a more specifically Scandinavian approach to the first meal of the day.

Note: all the recipes in this chapter are rendered as a set of instructions, more method than the recipe in the traditional parlance of cookbooks. Read through each step carefully before gathering ingredients and beginning to cook.

Rugbrød: Danish Rye Bread

Makes two loaves

This traditional recipe seems a bit intimidating at first, but once you get past the list of ingredients and become accustomed to making a sourdough starter, this is a delicious and hearty bread for any time of the day.

Stir together with a scant cup each of cracked rye kernels, cracked wheat, flax seeds, and sunflower seeds. To that, add 1 ½ cups of sourdough starter (there are many simple ways to make this, using just yeast, flour, and water - the internet has a variety of recipes), 3 cups of water, and 1-2 tablespoons of malted syrup (molasses will do in a pinch). Combine all these ingredients in the evening before you plan to bake your loaves, letting everything soak for about 8 hours or so.

The next morning, add 1 ½ cups each of rye flour and all-purpose flour, along with 1 tablespoon of salt. Let the dough rise for about 1-½ hours.

Bake the loaves in two standard loaf pans in a pre-heated oven at 350 degrees for about an hour. Take your loaves from the loaf pans, allowing them to cool a bit before slicing and slathering with butter or salted/sweetened yogurt or jam.

Porridge: Staple Food

Though many things could be named the national dish of Denmark, porridge would most certainly be in the running. There are as many recipes for porridge as there are Danes themselves! Here is one simple take on this classic staple, quite above and beyond the microwave oatmeal of American childhood.

For *one serving*, stir together about 4 ½ ounces of oatmeal (or other hearty grain, such as farro, spelt, or quinoa - cooking times will vary, of course) with a cup of water in a small saucepan. Add a cored and diced apple and ½ cup of berries (blueberries, blackberries, raspberries), along with 1/3 cup of chopped nuts, almond, pecans, or walnuts work well. Throw in a pinch or two of salt and let simmer until thickened and grains are tender. Once off the heat, serve with a few splashes of milk or cream - or a dollop of yogurt - and add a touch more salt for a savory take. You might add a little honey for sweetness.

As you can see, this recipe is most definitely a basic method to build according to your own tastes and what happens to be in your pantry or fridge. In keeping with the tradition of frugality, the Danes also like to make porridge out of stale rugbrød, with raisins, dried citrus peel, honey, and warming spices.

Ebleskivers: Danish Pancakes

Makes about three dozen

These fluffy pancake-like creations could be served for afternoon tea - or fika, as it is commonly called in Denmark - as well as breakfast. While there is a special ebleskiver pan to encourage these cakes to retain a biscuit-like shape and help them rise, you can easily cook them in a skillet or on a griddle like traditional American-style pancakes.

Whisk together 2 cups of flour, a teaspoon each of baking powder and baking soda, a generous pinch of salt, and a ¼ teaspoon of cinnamon in a large mixing bowl. Set this aside while you prepare the wet ingredients.

In another mixing bowl, beat 3 egg whites until they form stiff peaks - this will help the ebleskivers rise and contribute to their lightness.

In another bowl, beat the 3 egg yolks with a couple of tablespoons of sugar until incorporated, and then slowly beat in 2 cups of buttermilk and 2 teaspoons of vanilla. Mix in your dry ingredients, and then gently fold in your beaten egg whites.

For each small pancake, use a rounded tablespoon of batter. To each, add a teaspoon of finely diced fruit - peeled apples are the most traditional, but you can also use peaches, pears, or even small berries. Cook on a well-oiled griddle, skillet, or in an ebleskiver pan until the edges start to bubble and bottoms begin to lightly brown. Flip and cook for a minute more, then serve dusted with powdered sugar or topped with a dollop of whipped cream.

Lunch and Lighter Fare

Lunch is usually a lighter affair in Denmark, coming as it does between the two cherished traditions of a hearty, warming breakfast and the afternoon delights of the café for fika (coffee and a sweet snack). The recipes below provide just a quick sample of what might be on the menu, but there are innumerable variations on these themes. The category of smørrebrød itself is merely a blank canvas for any number of ingredients, and the popularity of soup provides a dizzying array of options, from pumpkin/squash to cauliflower to split pea – the list goes on! In addition, lunch might also be a hearty vegetable casserole or a savory variation on porridge. Lots of popular American fare could be considered a very hygge lunch: macaroni and cheese, for example, or a big bowl of pasta with ragu or pesto, or the ever-popular chicken pot pie; these are all warming, simple-yet- delicious meals that are very much in keeping with the spirit of hygge.

Smørrebrød: Infinite Variety

Smørrebrød essentially refers to an open-faced sandwich, usually eaten with knife and fork, topped with a nearly infinite variety of meats, cheeses, vegetables, and so on. These lunchtime treats are inescapably linked to Scandinavian countries, where they are a symbol of the simplicity and conviviality of the various peoples who reside there. Start with a decently thick slab of good bread – your choice, though rye is traditional for most smørrebrød – then slather with some rich butter, topping it all with favored ingredients. Some combinations you might enjoy trying:

Cold-smoked salmon with thinly sliced cucumber and lots of chopped, fresh dill

Sliced hard-boiled egg with avocado spears and thinly sliced radishes

Pickled herring or liver pâté with thinly sliced red onion and chopped parsley

Some good Havarti cheese with sliced tomato and chopped chives

Cured meats, such as salami or ham, with onions, tomatoes, and/or herbs

In short, just about anything you have in your fridge and/or garden would work in these open-faced sandwiches. Just don't forget the smear of butter and the heartiness of toppings. After all, these are knife-and-fork affairs.

Tomato Soup, Nordic Style

8-10 servings

Most - and I mean 99.99 percent - of American kids have enjoyed the lunchtime staple of hot tomato soup with grilled cheese. It's a classic, whether made from a can of Campbell's soup with Wonder Bread and a plastic-wrapped slice of cheese, or from some roasted garden tomatoes with local sourdough bread wrapped around artisanal cheddar. It's also very, very hygge: warm, comforting, familiar, simple, and delightfully delicious. The following recipe is a more Danish style take on that classic combo.

> Chop 1 onion, 2 or 3 cloves of garlic, a scant half pound of celeriac (celery root), and a couple of carrots, then sauté together in a large pot in 3 tablespoons olive oil until everything is softened a bit.
>
> Add 3 cups of chopped tomatoes (canned will work just fine), 2 tablespoons of tomato paste, 1 cup wine (usually a dry white, but you can experiment), and about 8 cups of stock. Homemade stock is always best, of course, but whatever you have the time for; remember that this is hygge

cooking and we are not supposed to be stressing about it! For a more traditional or vegan version, consider using vegetable or mushroom stock.

 Simmer everything together until all vegetables are cooked through and tender and the soup thickens slightly about ten or fifteen minutes. Serve either with cooked rye berries stirred in, or with a couple of thick slices of rugbrød, slathered with butter or topped with Edam cheese and broiled.

Hot Smoked Salmon: Scandinavian Staple

Serves 4

Salmon, along with herring, are also clear markers of Scandinavian food, ubiquitous throughout the region. Cold smoked salmon is best left to the experts unless you have the specialized equipment, but hot smoked salmon can be easily made in a home kitchen. Pair this with a nice green salad, and you have a satisfying meal.

Make a cure for one pound of salmon. You can use any kind of fish, like a firm, fatty fish such as like steelhead trout, but skin-on sockeye is perhaps most popular. Combine 2 cups of brown sugar with 1 cup kosher salt, 1 tablespoon of freshly ground black pepper, and a teaspoon each of ground coriander seed and juniper berries. *Optional: add grated zest from a couple of oranges for bright sweetness.* Let cure in the refrigerator for a couple of hours.

Set up your smoker. There are inexpensive, commercially available stovetop smokers which are very easy to use, and these are worth the small investment if you think you'll do this more than a couple of times a year. They are also great for smoking shellfish, tomatoes, and other vegetables, as well as small pieces of meat. If you don't have one, then create a makeshift smoker using a heavy pan with a lid, some aluminum foil, and some wood chips or dried tea leaves. To do this, put a layer of aluminum foil in your pan then scatter your wood chips over this layer. You can use tea and whole spices with the chips or instead of the chips; either way imparts flavor to your meat/fish. On top of the chips or spices, put down another layer of tin foil. Put your salmon into a steamer basket or tray, lower into the smoker, and cover with the lid. Turn your stove's heat to high and watch, with lid ajar, until you see wisps of smoke coming from the pan. Cover tightly, turn heat to medium so as not to burn your chips too quickly. Smoked your salmon for about 40 minutes until it flakes easily with a fork. If you like, baste a few times with some maple syrup for a lacquered look and a sweeter taste.

Café: Living the Fika Life

The importance of café culture to Denmark and other Scandinavian countries cannot be overstated; fika describes a daily ritual to take an afternoon break and meet with friends for coffee or cocoa and a quick snack. Cakes of all kinds are very common, as are various pastries and other sugary delicacies. As with many Danish foods, there is often a healthy dose of warming spices, such as cinnamon and cardamom, to be found in many traditional desserts. It is worth noting that many of the cakes, puddings, and pastries featured in cafes are also served for dessert - and breakfast.

Sugar Buns: Nearly No Effort Cinnamon Buns

Makes 12

Essentially, the following is a tasty recipe that has been hygge-fied into simplicity. Traditional cinnamon rolls take yeast and rising time and more complicated baking methods. These sugar buns can be made with easily purchased ingredients in the space of about half an hour. These are so easy and versatile that you'll likely have them on hand regularly once you try them.

Make some cinnamon sugar: combine 2 tablespoons each of granulated sugar and dark brown sugar (pack it tightly when measuring), a teaspoon of cinnamon, and a pinch of salt. Set aside while you prepare the dough.

Sprinkle a tablespoon of granulated sugar onto a work surface, then unfold one sheet of already prepared and thawed - but still cold - puff pastry over this. Thaw in the refrigerator overnight for best results. You can also use an equal amount of other purchased doughs, such as crescent roll or biscuit dough (2 cans worth) or a pound of pizza dough. Spread 2 tablespoons of softened butter over dough, then sprinkle with a third of your cinnamon-sugar mixture; pat lightly or press lightly with a rolling pin to be sure that sugar sticks to dough, then roll up tightly, starting with long end. Cut into 6 equal portions. Repeat with remaining dough, saving the last third of cinnamon sugar for sprinkling on top.

Place portions cut side up into buttered muffin tin wells, and then bake at 400 degrees for 20-25 minutes, until puffed and lightly browned. Melt another 4 tablespoons of butter, brush over the top of baked buns, and then sprinkle with reserved cinnamon sugar. Unmold from the pans while they are still warm.

Risalamande: Danish Rice Pudding

Serves Six

Rice pudding is a beloved dessert the world over, and the Danish do it especially well. Risalamande is traditionally served as a dessert at Christmas; however, a simpler version of it is eaten year-round. The Christmas version is dressed up with a cherry sauce if you'd like to splurge, but the basic recipe is just as tasty for an everyday treat.

Bring 1-¼ cups of water to a boil, then add 1-2/3 cups of short grain rice, and let boil for a couple of minutes. Stir in a split vanilla bean pod and 7 cups of whole milk; bring back to a boil, then cover and lower heat, simmering for 15 to 20 minutes, stirring occasionally, until rice is just past al dente stage. Remove from heat and discard the vanilla pod.

Transfer cooked rice to a bowl, and stir in 2 tablespoons granulated sugar, a teaspoon of salt, and the scraped seeds from another vanilla bean pod. Whip 2 cups heavy cream until soft peaks form, then fold gently into rice pudding, in three batches. Add 1-¼ cups chopped blanched almonds. At Christmas time, it is traditional to hide a whole blanched almond in the pudding, where some lucky diner will find it and be granted good fortune throughout the year. Taste for sweetness, correct if necessary, and then chill.

For extra decadence and a beautiful presentation, make a cherry sauce for topping! Start by simmering 1-½ pounds of pitted cherries (you can use frozen for ease) with ¾ cup of granulated sugar, another split vanilla bean pod, and 2 cups of water. Simmer for about 15 minutes, then mix 3 tablespoons of cornstarch with 2 tablespoons of water and stir this slurry into your cherry mixture. Cook until it thickens nicely, about 5 more minutes. Taste to see if it's sweet enough for your liking. Serve the cold pudding topped with hot cherry sauce for a lovely contrast in flavors, textures, and temperatures.

Sticky Chocolate Cake: Because Everyone Needs Chocolate

Serves six to eight people

A Scandinavian version of what we call - though a misnomer – "flourless chocolate cake" or "lava cake," this is a satisfyingly decadent dessert treat - and still quite simple - that just begs a cup of coffee to go with it.

Combine ½ cup flour with ¼ cup cocoa powder and a generous pinch of salt. Beat two eggs with 1-¼ cups of granulated sugar, then add dry mixture. Drizzle in ½ cup of melted butter and 1 tablespoon of vanilla, then pour into a greased 8-inch pie pan.

Back in the lower rack of a 300-degree oven for about half an hour. The center should be slightly set; it may take an additional five minutes or so, depending on the accuracy of your oven. Let the cake set up for an hour in the pan, then serve while still slightly warm or refrigerate for a fudgy treat the next day. This is probably not complete without some freshly whipped cream (or a scoop of ice cream) and some fresh berries.

Dinner: Slow-Cooked and Homemade

One of the attributes of hygge is to slow down and take your time to be present in your daily life, enjoying the little things as they come your way. Dinnertime is the perfect chance to take it low and slow, making a dinner that is both nutritious and indulgent, satisfying and hearty. A quick trip to the market and a few hours of patient waiting - during which you are engaging in activities with your kids, conversation with your friends, or wrapped up by the hearth reading a book - fill the home with wonderful and comforting smells, followed by a delicious dinner with family and friends. There are many traditional dinner foods that are classic hygge treats, such as the famed Swedish meatballs (made all over Scandinavia) or warming stews and big bowls of dumplings. There are any number of classic multicultural favorites in American cuisine that would easily qualify as hygge, from Italian lasagna or spaghetti and meatballs to Irish beef stew and soda bread to Chinese hotpot or Middle Eastern mezze to typical Midwestern casserole dishes, like Minnesota's famed hot dish. Basically, for a dinner to be hygge, it must be hearty and wholesome, simple and satisfying, not overly complicated or time-consuming, giving everyone time for togetherness and fellowship.

Braised Short Ribs: Timeless Classic

Serves 4-6

Just about every culture has some version of a long-cooked braise, and these short ribs are found all over countries with cold climes and cattle. The preparation time is reasonable, and the rest is merely patience and sides. These can be served on a bed of mashed potatoes, or better yet, mashed potatoes spiked with celeriac (celery root), mashed or roasted rutabagas or another turnip, or over a bed of buttered noodles. Add a quick green salad, and you have a full meal.

The very simplest version of this is to make a mirepoix of two diced onions, three carrots, and three stalks of celery, sautéed in olive oil for a few minutes. Add roughly six pounds of bone-in beef short ribs, a couple of bay leaves, and a bottle of red wine or 4 cups stock or water (or a combination to equal 4-5 cups), then cover and cook in a 325 degree oven for 3 or 4 hours, until the ribs are fall off the bone tender. But there are several variations and/or additions that will add flavor and sophistication to the dish:

Brown your short ribs on all sides before you add the mirepoix, scraping up the browned bits on the bottom of the pan, which add layers of flavor. Brown ribs in batches so that you avoid steaming them, then sauté mirepoix before returning ribs to pot (a Dutch oven is best).

Soak an ounce of dried mushrooms in hot water for half an hour, then chop and add to mirepoix for heightened umami (savory depth) of flavor.

Speaking of umami, for another boost you can add a tablespoon of anchovy paste, soy sauce, or fish sauce along with mirepoix.

Add some sprigs of fresh rosemary or other appropriate dried herbs (oregano, thyme, winter savory) and some chopped garlic for extra flavor notes.

As with many braises, this is often even better the next day; letting the braise rest overnight in the refrigerator also gives you control over how fatty and flavorful the sauce is. After the braise is cooled, refrigerate overnight, then skim off hardened fat, and separate meat from liquid (you can shred the meat at this point, if you like, depending on how you will serve it). Strain liquid and adjust seasonings or add the slurry to thicken it to pour over the finished dish.

Hasselback Potatoes: Vegetarian Delight

Serves 4

Having a hygge meal doesn't always preclude vegetarians. While Denmark is certainly a meat-eating country (as most northern European countries are), it is certainly forward-thinking in terms of health and can be vegetarian-friendly. These lovely potatoes, versions of which are served all over Scandinavia, are one such dish that is hearty enough to be a main, served alongside a green salad, and perhaps some roasted sprouts or braised cabbage.

Basically, these are baked potatoes that are fanned out in order to create a more browned interior and slightly more interesting texture and look than a regular baked potato. Take four large baking potatoes and cut small horizontal slits in them along the length of the potato; the idea is to leave the potato whole, so don't cut all the way through to the bottom. The best way to do this is to position the potato between two wooden-handled spoons (or chopsticks), then to cut until the knife hits the barrier. You want the cuts to be as close as possible, about ¼ to 1/8 of an inch apart. Wrap prepped potatoes in foil, then bake in a 400-degree oven for about 40 minutes (depending on the size of the potato, this may take longer). Unwrap the potatoes and brush all over and in between slits with olive oil (vegan version) or melted butter, and season well with salt and pepper. Return to oven, unwrapped, and bake for an additional 15 or 20 minutes.

If you'd like to fancy these up a bit - a nice idea (especially if they are to be the main course) is to then add some slices of cheese. Gruyere would be fantastic here, or crumbles of blue cheese placed between the slits. Then return the potatoes to the oven briefly, allowing your cheese slices t to melt. To keep it vegan, add some chopped fresh chives, parsley, and garlic to add some oomph. Use your imagination, as well, if you're not restrained by dietary needs: you could stuff the slits with thinly sliced ham and Swiss cheese, or in a nod to Jansson's temptation, some chopped anchovies.

Pork and Christmas Cabbage: Special Occasion

6 servings

Flaeskesteg is a popular and festive dish at Christmas, and while it is still quite simple to prepare, it does take some planning to track down a good piece of pork with the skin still attached. Christmas cabbage is a brilliantly hued dish of pickled red cabbage that is traditionally served on Christmas Eve. The wonderful thing about both recipes is that they are so truly simple while being very special.

The hardest part about the pork dish is finding a nice pork roast with the skin on; you may have to special order this if you don't live near a good butcher or a well-stocked market. In any case, you'll want a 5-7-pound pork roast with skin on. Score the skin all over, being careful not to cut into the meat below. Put the pork on a rack in a roasting pan that has been stocked with a quartered onion or two, some sprigs of rosemary and/or thyme, and a cup of water. The drippings from the pork will combine with the aromatics below to create the base for a simple sauce if you like. Rub the pork all over with butter and season generously with salt.

Roast the pork for about two hours at 400 degrees, making sure that the liquid in the roasting pan never quite runs out. When the roast is done, strain the drippings and skim off the fat; reserve to make the sauce. Before serving, return the roast to the oven under the broiler for a few minutes, to crisp up the skin - be careful not to let this burn.

Meanwhile, make the sauce: boil the strained skimmed drippings for a few minutes until slightly thickened. Add a couple of splashes of cream to this with salt and pepper to taste. For added flavor, crumble is some blue cheese or add a couple of tablespoons of tart jelly, such as red currant.

For the Christmas cabbage, simmer a shredded head of red cabbage, 2 cups each granulated sugar and white vinegar, 3 cups of water, and 2 teaspoons of salt in a large pot for about an hour. Leftovers are excellent, served cold on a sandwich.

Warming Drinks

Finally, any day that is filled with the hygge spirit will also include some warming drinks, no matter the time of year. Certainly, wintertime sees more cocoa made and spiced (and spiked) drinks abound, but coffee is ubiquitous throughout the year in Danish homes and cafes, and tea is also gaining a foothold in this more globalized climate. No breakfast or trip to the café would be complete without a warming drink. Expand your repertoire with the following recipes.

Hot and Spicy Cocoa

Serves 12 (or 6 twice, if you're having a really hygge day)

For the hot chocolate mix, combine a cup each of unsweetened cocoa powder and granulated sugar, a tablespoon of cinnamon, and ½ teaspoon each of ground ginger and nutmeg (freshly grated is great, but whatever you have on hand will do). For extra flavor, add a pinch or two of ground cardamom and, for more spice, add ½ teaspoon of ground chipotle powder. For each serving, use 3 tablespoons of the mixture stirred into 1 ½ cups of hot milk, preferably whole milk.

Another bonus: use vanilla sugar for some of your sugar mixes. This is easy to make from home with the spent pods of vanilla beans that you've used to make the rice pudding above. Just bury the pods in some sugar in a tightly sealed jar (thoroughly washed old mayonnaise or pickle jars are great for this). Shake every few days. After a couple of weeks, the sugar will be redolent of vanilla. Use in your coffee, too. Keep topping up with more sugar and spent pods as you go, making sure to distribute everything evenly, to keep a steady supply on hand.

Berry Merry Glögg

Serves 8-10

Mulled wines of all kinds are popular throughout the cold climates of Europe. This one is special because of the addition of berries and rum.

Simmer 4 cups of blackberries, blueberries, raspberries, or a combination thereof with ¼ to ½ cup of sugar, depending on how sweet you want the resulting drink to be, for about 10 minutes, until broken down and thickened. Puree with 3 cups of water in blender or food processor and push through a sieve.

Return the sieved puree to the pot and add your aromatics: zest from one orange (in a thick spiral), a couple of cinnamon sticks and star anise pods, some cardamom seeds, a split vanilla bean pod, and some cloves. Simmer this for 20 minutes or so, keeping the lid on to avoid excess evaporation. Add a bottle of red wine to this, along with some rum to taste; a generous splash is about right, but too little and it has no impact. Too much, and it overwhelms with alcohol. Heat this very gently so you don't boil off the alcohol, then ladle into mugs, leaving whole spices behind. Some people add raisins and blanched nuts to this, as well, for a warm drink and a snack all in one.

Mulled Cider

8 servings

This is made based on the same principles above, but it is simpler and can be either alcoholic or non-alcoholic.

Simmer two quarts of cider (again, alcoholic or not, depending on your desire) with a couple of cinnamon sticks, the zest of an orange, some cloves, and either cardamom pods or allspice berries. When warm and fragrant, serve in nice thick mugs.

Chapter 7: Practical Hygge: Hygge Holidays and Seasons

While hygge is most definitely associated with the Christmas holiday season and winter, it is certainly possible to practice hygge any time of the year. Indeed, as this philosophy becomes more popular across the globe, many people are applying hygge principles to holidays, festivals, and seasonal activities throughout the year. Of course, the Danes would suggest that this is quite right, as hygge is a mindset - not a passing mood. Any day is a good day for hygge, and throughout this chapter, you will find ideas for how to keep yourself engaged with the hygge spirit.

Winter: Hyggelige Season!

For too many of us, winter is a time to dread, with cold and blustery weather, complicated travel, holiday pressures, bored or sick kids stuck indoors at home. For the Danish people who embrace the philosophy of hygge, wintertime can be the most magical, comforting, coziest time of year. The essence of hygge truly embodies what we most love about wintertime: wrapping yourself in a blanket in front of a fire, wearing cozy socks, cooking comforting foods, and taking some time off your busy schedule for a little relaxing self-care and family celebration. No time of year is better suited for indulging in hygge. Some ideas for how to hygge up your winter follow below.

Since you can't spend too much time outside, bring nature inside: potted poinsettias are a holiday tradition that both brightens and soothes your home sanctuary.

If you do spend time outdoors, invest in (or make) a firepit; there's nothing more hygge than gathering around a roaring fire and roasting marshmallows with friends and family.

Also, don't forget about winter sports: if you're lucky enough to live where there's adequate snowfall, take the family out for sledding, skiing, or ice skating. These are excellent ways to bond as a family and make the best out of the colder weather while getting some healthy outdoor activity.

Consider a nighttime trek through the snow - with or without snowshoes, depending on your area – as there is nothing quite so magical as the glint of moonlight on freshly fallen snow.

If the cold eventually gets you down, take refuge in a café. You were going to anyway, right? That's a daily activity! Bump it up a notch, and instead of your regular haunt, visit a museum and take your afternoon fika in their café; most larger museums now have a small eating place on the grounds.

Create your own visual memories, taking out your camera to get some pictures of nature and family. Put together an album to share with everyone.

Don't forget about our fellow creatures - it's cold out there for everyone! Put out some food or a feeder for the birds and spend some hygge time watching and learning - an excellent way to involve kids in naturalist activities.

Think of your home bathroom like a spa retreat: invest in some bubble bath or bath salts, put on some relaxing music, and have a warm and fluffy robe waiting for you at the end of a soothing bath.

Remember that wintertime foods are not limited to holidays. There is no better time of year to indulge in a daily cup of cocoa than winter, breaking out the old fondue pot, and inviting your friends for a party. Be sure to have some mulled wine or cider on hand, as well.

Tackle the stack of books on your nightstand: set up a hyggekrog (cozy nook) and indulge in some blissful hours of pleasurable reading. And, by the way, real books with some heft are far more hyggelige than reading on an electronic device. Just saying...

Have a pajama day where the whole family stays in and lounges about, ideally indulging in both group activities. Board games, anyone? Movie marathon with popcorn and sweets? If not a group gathering, each can snuggle in with books.

Start a treasure jar. Though this can be done at any time of the year, it's particularly potent during winter to see how nature changes from fall into spring. Collect small items from your daily walk or bike ride (you know, your hygge activity) and store them in a jar. At the end of the season, arrange and display your newfound treasures.

Learn something new or teach something new - or both. Cook with your children, enroll in a class about something you've always wanted to learn, or teach yourself a different language.

Do some stargazing - figuratively and literally. Make plans for the next season, drawing up your dream garden for the spring, thinking about your summer vacation, etc. Be sure not to forget to look up into the clear night sky and treasure the present (gratitude!) and dream of the future.

Christmas *Is* the Most Wonderful Hyggelige Time of the Year

In mainly Christian countries of the north, the holiday most associated with wintertime is Christmas. With this holiday comes a host of traditions that are very hyggelige - in fact, the very notion of upholding and creating tradition is part of the hygge spirit itself. Even if you celebrate another seasonal holiday (for example, Hanukkah or Kwanzaa), you can adapt some of these traditions for your own enjoyment.

Lights, lights, and more lights! Fairy lights or twinkle lights can adorn every room in the house, along with candles and Christmas tree lights. Put them in clear jars or string them across bookshelves or wrap around railings.

Write letters to Santa with your children. Encourage them to think of these letters not just as personal wish lists of material objects, but also of lists about what to be thankful for and what to look forward to in the new year.

Decorate the house both inside and out with seasonal objects: reindeers and trees, elves and snowmen, lights and ornaments, wreaths and garlands. Make it a family activity and involve everyone in creating a special environment for a special time of year.

Host a wrap party, either with family or friends (or both). Have everyone develop their own special skill, whether it be coordinating paper and ribbon, making bows, or using special lettering for gift cards.

Make homemade gifts: jams and jellies, pickles and preserves, liqueurs and flavored libations are all welcome hostess gifts this time of year. If you have other skills, use these as well: sketch a drawing, paint a picture, or write and frame a poem. Pottery and woodworking crafts are also fabulous. These kinds of handmade gifts are truly priceless.

Go and see a Christmas show with the family, whether it be local production of The Nutcracker or the latest Christmas-themed movie. While you're at it, listen to some carols or take the family caroling around the neighborhood.

Start a new tradition to return to each year: decorate personalized mugs for every member of the family; knit hats or scarves for friends, give dated ornaments to the special people in your life, host a marathon holiday movie weekend or have Christmas Eve brunch for neighbors and friends.

Spring: Renew and Re-energize

After the comforts (and challenges) of winter pass, many people look forward to the spring. It is naturally the time of year when our thoughts turn to renewal and rebirth; the birds start singing again, the earth awakens, and we return to the outdoors with renewed vigor. All these typical springtime feelings are completely compatible with the philosophy of hygge: working outdoors, playing outdoors, observing and respecting nature, feeling gratitude for the little miracles in our everyday lives, cozying up to a fulfilling project that allows us to spend time with family and friends. We may trade in our oversize sweaters for lighter cardigans and put the cozy socks and fire-building on hold for the moment, but there is nothing that says we must put our hygge mindset on pause. Some of the ways in which you can keep up your hyggelige practice are as follows:

First and foremost, don't abandon your candles! There is nothing that says pretty in spring like small tea candles on a picnic table or in your dining room. Choose fresh but muted colors, like peach and pale green for an acknowledgment of the awakening natural scene outdoors. This lighting, along with opening your windows and letting fresh air and natural light in, will keep you in the hygge spirit every day.

Flowers should also be a part of your hygge springtime. And, more importantly, these flowers should be natural flowers, found just outside your door - even the most humble-looking weed-like flower is beautiful in the right arrangement and under the right-minded gaze! Wildflowers in mason jars are evocative of springtime hygge in a surefire way.

Play in the dirt! One of the most marvelous things about springtime is the opportunity to get outside and get your hand dirty: plant a garden, build a treehouse, or put in some more trees or hedgerows. Build something for the future in the glorious weather of spring.

Speaking of the outdoors, be sure to go on a picnic or two, or ten, while the weather is perfect for such things. Fly a kite, play in the park, notice the ducklings hatching and the butterflies emerging. Introduce your children to the wonders of springtime rebirth.

Speaking of the outdoors in inclement weather be sure to play in the rain! A gentle springtime rainfall is one of the most beautiful feelings in the world, especially to a young child in all his wonderment. And if you live in an area that gets some fierce spring weather - and that's most of us - enjoy it like you enjoy the wintertime. Marvel; at the power of nature while you are inside your safe haven with loved ones. These are the days built for hyggekrogs and reading binges.

Look at your home décor and really think spring. Keep it minimalist and tidy, as hygge would have us do, but bring in a few lighter, somewhat brighter pieces to match the changing of the seasons outside. Put some fresh sheets on the bed and swap out your ultra-fuzzy robe for a sleek silk one to welcome in the warmer weather.

As to cooking, springtime hygge is all about the market. Get yourself to the local farmers' market and indulge in all the rare and fleeting springtime treats such as fresh strawberries and asparagus, fava beans and sugar snap peas, baby lettuces and delicate herbs, spring chickens and their glorious eggs. There's a reason why Easter feasts typically feature devilled eggs and young lamb - it's just the right season for it. Check out some more Easter ideas below.

Easter Redux

Perhaps the ultimate celebration of renewal and rebirth is the hallowed holiday of Easter. No matter how you celebrate it, Easter is a lovely springtime opportunity to gather with family and friends around a table laden with food, sharing gratitude for all we are fortunate to have. Even if you don't celebrate Easter, there is ample opportunity to initiate a secular springtime festival, with some or all the ideas below:

Secret snowdrop letters: this is a Danish tradition at Easter, to send a crafted paper letter to a loved one, with a sweet and caring message, left unsigned. The tradition says that, if the recipient guesses that you sent the letter, you must give them an Easter egg; if they cannot guess who sent it, then they must give you an Easter egg. It's kind of like a Secret Santa for springtime. The trick is to cut out a beautiful paper design, as you might have done (depending on your age) in school with hearts for Valentine's Day or a paper daisy chain.

In terms of holiday décor, many Danes will even put up a kind of Easter tree with spring branches and other material from nature. It is adorned with symbols of fertility (like eggs) and rebirth (like feathers and flowers).

Speaking of eggs, certainly any Easter celebration is bereft without the traditional dyed eggs, of course, but to be extra-hygge about it, choose natural dyes that come from common kitchen items rather than chemical ones (for example: beet juice or chlorophyll extract). And, of course, you'll be doing this with children, family, and/or friends around your dining table.

Have an Easter egg hunt but try to make sure it's outside. Sometimes spring weather prohibits this, as people in my region well know! Every other year, it seems that Easter is freezing and forbidding outside. Nevertheless, if possible, gather for the hunt outside. If not outside, no worries! The idea of a playful task for children is hygge in and of itself.

Don't forget to enjoy some special Easter treats, as well, the kinds of chocolate delights that come along only once a year - all the better if they are homemade, of course, but some purchased delicacies can become a yearly tradition, as well.

Speaking of food, an Easter feast is always in order! Indeed, it can be one of the most indulgent of the year and the food itself is hyggelige in its very nature: fresh spring vegetables, a big comforting ham or leg of spring lamb, lush devilled eggs (to make use of all those handsomely dyed ones), braided Easter bread, and luscious desserts. Be sure to have a lovely centerpiece made with natural spring branches and other found materials. And candles! And lots of family and friends.

Homemade Easter decorations are a treat and a way to practice hygge with your children and others. It is also very hyggelige to make gifts for your annual Easter baskets, whether they be edible or crafted - this shows how much you care for your kids or others to whom you give gifts.

And don't forget Mother's Day, another day to treat your mom to a hygge experience!

Summer: The Outdoors is Ours

Since every time of year is a time for hygge and since summer is the time for vacation, relaxation, and outdoor activities, you might say that this is the most hyggelige time of the year - outside of winter. Most people take some time off in the summer, and it is certainly the time of year for lots of friendly outside gatherings with fun and sun. It may not be cozy socks and blankets, but that doesn't mean that you can't hygge up your outdoor spaces and your indoor activities.

Lighten up your linens so you feel free to luxuriate in bed all morning long. In fact, why not treat yourself - or a loved one - to breakfast in bed? Make your bedroom a bright and welcoming space for exactly the kind of re-charging relaxation we could all use at any time of the year.

Use your sunroom - or make one, as best you can. Create a hyggekrog that gets the best sunlight and set up a comfy couch or lazy lounge chair in there with plenty of throw pillows, cushions, and natural lighting. This is the place to catch up on summer reading.

Speaking of summer reading, this is the time of year to indulge yourself in light, breezy reading, whatever that means to you: romantic comedies, mysteries, memoirs. Leave the studying to another time of year.

Experience backyard living as much as you can: make a space in your backyard where everyone feels comfortable gravitating toward. Make sure there are cozy seats, enough for everyone, and natural décor for all to enjoy.

Dine outside, of course, in your cozy backyard space, weather and bugs permitting. Put out some citronella to help with bugs to make it a safe space for everyone.

Put up a hammock and set out some deck chairs, because this is the time of year to lounge - preferably with a nice cup of tea or glass of wine. Part of the hygge spirit is to slow down and enjoy every day; this is the perfect environment in which to do just that.

Go camping and toast hot dogs and marshmallows around the campfire with your friends and family. If you're lucky, you'll have a beach nearby where you can enjoy a sunny day of fun and play followed by a warm night of good conversation and glorious summertime food.

Pick up shells along the beach and make a garland or a necklace or a centerpiece for your dining table back at home.

If you can, take a vacation. Better yet – and even more hyggelige – take a staycation, turning your home into a weekend or week-long getaway.

Finally, remember a key component of the hygge philosophy: it's not about the financial investment; it's about the experience itself.

Festival of Days, from Memorial to Labor

Summertime is also rife with potential celebratory holidays, most of them secular holidays enjoyed by most Americans. Memorial Day, at the end of May, semi-officially kicks off the summer season, followed by Father's Day in June and Independence Day in July. The summer season semi-officially ends with the Labor Day holiday at the beginning of September. Obviously, these celebrations are American-centric; however, any excuse to host a celebration or to practice hygge with family and friends is nearly always a good one. Consider some of the following ideas on how to hygge-fy your summer holidays:

Memorial Day is primarily a day of remembrance for fallen soldiers and veterans who have sacrificed much for our country; it is in the spirit of gratitude that we should approach the day. It is also the perfect time of year, weather-wise, to commune with family and friends at an outdoor gathering, usually a backyard barbecue. Spend the day putting flags and flowers at gravesites, attend a service for veterans, and/or visit your own family and friends who are veterans - this spirit of gratitude is very hygge. Then, spend the evening bonding with family and friends at a big backyard party, utilizing some of the tips mentioned above.

Father's Day is also a day to express gratitude toward fathers who raised and mentored you. Remember that we may all have more than our biological fathers to honor on a day like this; perhaps a cherish grandfather or uncle, an adoptive father or stepfather, or an important mentor. Make a homemade card or gift to send your father figure(s) and be sure to let them know how much they mean to you. This can often take the form of another backyard barbecue or other kind of family gathering where the food is simple, and the company is grand.

Independence Day is a celebration of America's history and independence, and another chance to express gratitude. It is also a chance to spend some time with family and friends and good food. Fireworks are perhaps a bit flashy for the normally subdued spirit of hygge, but in this case, the exuberance is well-placed. To make the fourth more hyggelige, give yourself a day at the beach, some time to reflect, and gather together with others in celebration. Also, grill some hygge food, like burgers and ribs!

Labor Day honors the hard work that we all put in throughout the year. You could easily argue that, if hygge were a more ingrained part of American culture, we wouldn't need a Labor Day holiday at all - every day would be a way to enjoy work-life balance. In any case, note that Labor Day is the end of one season and the beginning of another, usually busier, time of year. Honor this by reminding yourself that hygge practice can be followed throughout the year, even with school starting back up and the lazy days of summer over. The Labor Day holiday is the perfect time to commit yourself to the practice of hygge through the fall and into the glorious winter. It's also another wonderful excuse to drag out the grill for one last outdoor shebang.

Fall: Cozy Up

While fall can seem to some like the end of the extended vacation that is summer, for others - and that means us, with our hyggelige vision - it can represent the long, slow slide into the coziest of seasons. Fall weather is crisp, and we start to bring out our oversize sweaters and cozy socks. Fall colors are naturally beautiful, so we incorporate those into our home décor. Fall evenings are muted and calm, perfect for postprandial strolls. Fall is the season when shops begin to close up earlier, bringing us back into the safe havens of our homes. It's one of the loveliest times of the year. Some uniquely fall activities and ideas to bring more hygge into your season are listed below.

Do some fall planting: there are many crops and plants that like to spend the winter cozying up underground, so here is your last opportunity of the year to get your hands dirty in the yard and garden! Tulips are one such flower that likes to overwinter and are a beautiful symbol of spring. If you like vegetable gardens, then planting tubers and other root vegetables is the thing to do. Overwintering garlic is one of the most enjoyable - and simplest - kind of planting to do!

Think of the symbol of the cornucopia: fall is the time to show gratitude for abundance, the prolific harvest. Do some canning and preserving - don't waste the end-of-season abundance that you have all around you. Share your bounty with family, friends, and neighbors.

Go apple picking; get the family outdoors to enjoy the perfect time of year for this most symbolic of fruits. Have an apple bobbing contest later that evening, make some caramel apples for a divine fall treat - or both.

Take a road trip to enjoy the changing of the seasons and the outburst of fall colors. Be sure to pack a picnic or two for along the way and sit under a tree while you watch the leaves gently drift to the ground.

Welcome the pumpkin: one of the enduring symbols of fall, pumpkin and various other squash really come into their own this time of year. Aside from the whole jack-o-lantern business, you can also make pumpkin bread, pie, soup, and a whole host of other hyggelige recipes designed to make the best out of this hallowed vegetable.

Start your knitting or learn how: this is the time of year to start on your projects for winter and gift-giving season. More on this in Chapter 10.

Fall is also a wonderful time of year to take some photographs out in nature; the light is just right on most days, and the beautiful colors create gorgeous photos.

Host a scavenger hunt! Cleverer and more adult than Halloween, a scavenger hunt is the perfect fall activity for a group of game friends. Get outside, have some fun, then be sure to offer some big bowls of soup and hunks of crusty bread to enjoy - along with good conversation - at the end of the evening.

Thanksgiving Is Not Just for Americans

The fall season isn't as rife with holidays, secular or otherwise, as the other seasons. For Americans, Thanksgiving holds great importance: it is both a nationally celebrated holiday that crosses all religious and cultural lines, as well as official start to the grand holiday season that is winter. Even if you aren't American - or if you find the myth of Thanksgiving a little too whitewashed for your taste - you can still appreciate the underlying message of giving thanks for all that we have enjoyed throughout the year. For most Americans, Thanksgiving means certain foods and family gatherings, and that is certainly in the spirit of hygge, as well: tradition and gratitude are key components of living the hygge lifestyle. So, roast your turkey and stuffing, if you like, or simply have friends and family over for a potluck dinner. Either way, you are practicing the greatest simple joys of hygge.

Chapter 8: Practical Hygge: Hygge Parenting, Relationships, and Togetherness

One of the most crucial components in practicing hygge is to encourage and facilitate positive relationships, fostering togetherness. Practicing hygge can have a profound impact on all your relationships, from parenting with empathy to nurturing a spousal bond to becoming a better friend. The hyggelige traditions of communing in cafes and eating family dinners around a set table together create bonds of affection that are lifelong. Hygge activities also emphasize the importance of spending time with our loved ones with joy and attentiveness. Embracing the simplicity and pleasure of every day is profoundly comforting to all of us - especially children - and recognizing that our highest forms of happiness come from our relationships with others remains at the core of the hygge way of life.

Parents: Parenting Peacefully

The impact that we have as parents cannot be overstated, of course, and the way that we decide to parent not only affects the physical and psychological health of our children but it also serves as a model for how our children behave and interact with others out in the world. Eventually, in most cases, this transfers to how your children parent their own kids. The hygge way of parenting emphasizes togetherness, authenticity, and empathy. It may seem, at first glance, that the hygge lifestyle is for the carefree and childless: afternoons spent lounging in cafes or in front of a fire or reading binges in a cozy and quiet corner. Yet, the underlying values inherent to the concept of hygge can be applied quite appropriately to parenting styles. Who among us wouldn't embrace the idea of "peaceful parenting?" It may sound easier said than done, but with a few thoughtful tips and techniques, you can incorporate the best of hygge into your parenting style.

One of the most important parenting techniques you can employ is that of being present with your children. Tune in to their needs and wants, rather than trying to project onto them what you think they might need or want. Get down on their level - literally - and see the world through their eyes.

Be sincere and authentic when responding to their interests. Any child of reasonable acuity knows when an adult condescends to them, so respond with genuine questions and support.

Empathy is also a central tenant in hygge-style parenting (and living, in general); fostering an empathy of others by demonstrating this to your own children creates a bond like no other.

Encourage creative activity: get involved in art projects with your children or play dress-up or make-believe. Nurture their imagination and create a safe space for them to express themselves. Believe it or not, you will gain as much from this interaction as they do.

Encourage play that is stimulating to the senses. While technological devices and computers have a place in our lives, to be sure, there is something to be said for more traditional kinds of tactile play. Consider investing in a sandbox, make models, or play with dough.

Music is also an excellent way to get kids - and yourself - up and moving, while stimulating our bodies and minds. Physical activity is as important to brain development and overall health as is intellectual pursuits.

Always eat together and encourage your children to participate. This ritual cannot be stressed enough! This habit of spending time preparing food, giving thanks, and eating around a table together is a habit for life. Study after study shows the amazing benefits that this one simple ritual can have on children. It makes for more humane, empathetic, and grateful interactions for the rest of their lives.

Playing games together is another key component in fostering a child into adulthood. Games often provide practice for real life - at least in traditional games. With this in mind, try weaning kids away from the phone and the computer, engaging them in other forms of play that help them to model relationships and activities that will assist them in adulthood.

Don't forget to play outside, as well. Nurture a love of the outdoors and empathy for nature, in general. Remember the Danish saying: there is no bad weather, only bad clothing choices. Outdoor play is a year-round affair, and in any season, there is always the reward of returning to the safe haven of the home, either for a mug of cocoa and a bowl of soup or for some lemonade and a smørrebrød spread.

Read together - another surefire way to create a lifelong, positive habit! Encourage children to spend quiet time reading along, as well. Allow children the space to figure out their own self-care.

Spend some time with physical affection, too. Snuggling and comforting your children is one the most significant things you can do to make them feel safe and happy throughout their lives. When you give them your full attention and engagement, you give them peace and happiness.

Finally, remember to believe in yourself: trusting your hygge instincts as a parent will give you the confidence, kindness, and patience to nurture your children with love and generosity.

Partners: Nurturing Relationships

We would also do well to consider the foundations of a hygge lifestyle when approaching our partners, whether they are spouses, significant others, or co-parents. We often forget that relationships take effort, just as raising children to do. Without the same kind of nurturing spirit with which we approach our children, relationships can stagnate or grow untenable. The concept of hygge is easily applicable to our romantic relationships, and many of the basic tenants of hygge in and of themselves will foster a healthy connection. For example, creating a comforting and cozy home is a first step toward coming home from work into a welcoming environment, the kind of place where a good mood is easy to come by. Other tips and techniques for maintaining happy love relationships are as follows.

> Create good energy throughout your house, especially the places in which you interact at an intimate level, such as the bedroom. The living area is for everyone who enters your house, but the bedroom should be a place that is hygge-fied just for the two of you.

> Fill your home with items that have meaning, rather than material objects that simply advertise wealth or success. You can't buy hygge; instead, you build it via memory-making and attention to the mundane details of the everyday. Family

photographs, mementos from vacations, natural found objects decorate your space in such a way that cements togetherness.

But don't forget yourself. One of the foundational elements in creating a hygge relationship is to embody hygge ideals yourself. Self-care is necessary in order to care for anyone else. Also, think of this in terms of your house: it should remind you not only of your present togetherness, but also of your individual self. Losing yourself in a relationship is not a formula for happiness, but rather a recipe for long-term resentments.

Communication, as we all well know, is key to any constructive relationship. Learn to communicate openly, honestly, authentically, and calmly for best results.

Cooperation is also key to any successful relationship, especially if it involves multiple people and objectives: partners raising children together invariably must cooperate on many fronts, but you also must learn to cooperate within the confines of your one interpersonal relationship. This is reliant on open and honest communication and a desire to put togetherness ahead of other goals.

Leave work at work. This is harder to do than it sounds for many, if not most of us. However, if you are to create a relationship with true togetherness that embodies the spirit of hygge, then you must pay attention to the ways in which your working life invades your home life. Try to achieve as much balance as you can, and if you simply must address work issues at the home, try to follow some simple rules. Do not interrupt family time around the dinner table with work. Designate a specific area of the house - *not* the bedroom - in which work might be briefly conducted. Finish any work at least an hour before you plan to get to sleep, so you won't sacrifice evening bonding.

Speaking of dinner, that time is a sacred time, something to be protected and honored. Make it a habit to keep it sacred.

Use music to set the mood: curate your own playlists for different occasions, different seasons to keep you in the spirit of relaxed happiness.

Slowing down, in general, is the rule of thumb when practicing hygge. Make special time for your significant other daily, no matter how seemingly simple or limited this might be. Hold hands while watching a movie, take a walk after dinner, commit to an hour before bedtime alone without interruption.

Minimize the excess stuff in your lives, whether it is material or emotional. The baggage of all kinds interferes with peace and happiness.

Friends: Establishing Bonds

Another crucial factor in practicing hygge is to form and maintain friendship bonds. Besides your family, friends are the most important connections you have in the world, and ideally, friends fulfill needs that family cannot. Talking to a friend about the stresses you have in raising children is quite different than having that same discussion with a co-parent. Having some time away from family is just as healthy and important as spending quality time with them. Friendships are our way of keeping a sense of our own self separate from the needs and desires of family members. And, just as with children and with intimate relationships, friendships must be nurtured and cultivated with warmth and attention to maintain. One of the most striking facts to emerge out of recent sociological research is that social connection is the best predictor of overall happiness. Thus, we need to establish and maintain the bonds we have with our strongest social connections via friendships and other extended relationships.

Make time to spend with friends on a regular basis. It's wonderful if you can establish a standing date and time to meet with friends each week or create a ritual in which friendly interactions take place with spontaneity and ease.

The café culture in Denmark creates a kind of built-in experience in which to foster friendships; if you don't have that kind of thing where you live, think of other places/ways in which friendly meetings can happen (a diner, a bookshop, a casual bar).

Invest in friendships by welcoming them into your home: host a monthly Sunday brunch, or Saturday game night, or Friday night card game, or wine Wednesdays, or thirsty Thursdays - whatever works best for your crowd. The point is to make the event a recurring one rather than an occasional one; planning and fuss are kept to a minimum, and your house becomes the welcoming, comforting place to be.

Encourage drop-ins. This is not a typically American attitude in our contemporary society, where we often don't even know our neighbors, but this is an ingrained part of Danish life. If your home is hygge-fied, then you may find that it happens anyway.

Don't worry about throwing big, elaborate parties in order to bond with friends. Oftentimes, the most intimate bonding happens with just a handful of people, ideally being three to five. Also, this isn't the point of hyggelige togetherness anyway; the point is to be relaxed, a comfortable, and casual wherein great company can be readily enjoyed.

But do always have good food and drinks on hand. This doesn't have to be fancy, to reiterate, but in the spirit of hospitality, honor your friends with generosity and kindness.

Savor the moment: envision time with friends as you would time with family, a time to unplug from devices and to interact with conviviality and conversation.

Remember that friendship is a choice, unlike family, and with those choices come a dedication to caring for others outside of your immediate family. This kind of thinking has a definite ripple effect, radiating out from family to friends to neighbors to strangers. Fostering mutual respect and empathetic connection among peoples is at the heart of practicing hygge.

Family: Intergenerational Togetherness

Everything that can be said above about friendship and most of what can be said about our family relationships also applies to extended family. One of the tragedies of modern American life is that we spend more time with technology than ever and less time with our extended families and elders. So much wisdom is to be gained from maintaining relationships and connection with our grandparents, aunts, uncles, mentors, and others. While this is certainly not relegated just to hygge practice, the relationships that we can foster with extended family members enrich, enlighten, and enliven our lives in innumerable ways.

A story that might illustrate this better than any is that of a young woman who was going off to college, only to find that her scholarships didn't quite cover the cost of living on campus. Her grandmother lived nearby, but the prospect of spending her undergraduate years in her grandmother's home was not the most appealing - this wasn't how she envisioned college, for sure! Having no alternative, though, she acquiesced and moved her stuff into the guest room in the back. It was difficult at first, for though she had always spent time with this grandmother growing up, she had never been particularly close to her. Unlike her other grandmother, who doted on her and did grandmotherly things like baking and crafts, this grandmother was more interested in friends, cards, and adult conversation.

Much to her surprise when, gradually over time, she began to understand where her grandmother had come from: a rural and very poor background during which her father died young, leaving her uneducated mother to raise five children on her own. She learned that her grandmother had to take work as a young woman, foregoing further education, to support herself, and fell in love with an older man - her grandfather - who had old-fashioned ideas about women working outside the house. Her grandmother, she came to discover, was a wicked smart and fun-loving person who had never been afforded the opportunities in life to develop all she could have been. Instead, she now spent her days tirelessly supporting her granddaughter's endeavors to achieve all that she had been denied.

It dawned on the granddaughter one day that her grandmother was no mere grandmother: she was a mentor, a protective mothering figure, and a best friend. That relationship impacted the way she would view relationships from there on, with empathy and joy in the discovery of connection where it didn't seem that one could exist. That was the hygge spirit of the grandmother: she took pleasure in the small things in life, cooked with gusto, welcomed with open arms, and fostered love and happiness in all those she cared for. It would do us all good to take some time to foster those kinds of connections with our elders, if for nothing else than to teach us how to embrace hygge practice in the face of anything the world throws at us.

Chapter 9: Practical Hygge: Frugal Hygge

It has been stated repeatedly throughout this book that practicing hygge does not require lavish expenditures. It is not about money; it is about the experience. Indeed, one of the very tenants of hygge is to avoid waste and enjoy what exists within the realm of your daily life - simplicity, simplicity, simplicity! Beyond this, however, there are ways to think about hygge as the happiest kind of frugal life you can lead. Anyone can practice hygge, no matter what their income and certain activities that are inherently hygge are also inherently budget-friendly. Check out some money-saving tips for how to hygge well and within a budget.

The Checklist

What about all those candles? First, don't spend a fortune on them, whatever you do! It's hard to practice hygge right without them, and you'll inevitably burn through many, especially in winter. Shop the discount section of department stores for good bargains or seek out places where you can buy in bulk. Oftentimes, tea light and votive candles are a mere few cents each. In addition, eating (or living) by candlelight will invariably save you money on your electric bill. Marshalls™ always has a nice selection of candles and other hyggelige items - blankets, throw pillows, and the like - for reasonable prices. Wayfair.com is an online source for buying candles in bulk for more than half off-retail prices.

What is one of the most hyggelige activities you can do? *Stay at home.* You don't need to seek out entertainment and transportation. Invite friends over for drinks and a movie, no expensive cocktails or Uber required unless those friends are having more than one or two drinks and intend to drive home. One of the core concepts of hygge is to be cozy, comfortable, and happy inside your own home.

While you're at home, light up the fireplace or fire pit: this is an excellent way to stay warm and cozy for not a lot of money. Again, you are saving on gas or electricity while creating a cozy atmosphere for everyone to enjoy.

Invest in just a few good, sturdy mugs for drinks at home with friends - coffee, cocoa, glogg, mulled wine, cider, and so on are all lovely in a plain old mug. Again, buy in bulk (inevitably, one or two will get broken), and don't worry about fancy labels or delicate china. Something that will easily go into the dishwasher and feel warm and solid in your hands suits the bill perfectly. This is a good way to get started with creating a hygge feeling on a limited budget. Worry about the other pieces as you are able.

Decorate with natural and/or "found" objects. There is no need to spend a lot of money - or any, really - to create a hygge aesthetic in your home. Branches, pebbles, dried flowers and leaves arranged and displayed nicely are all you need to bring a little hygge home. All the better if you "craft" them up a bit. See the next chapter for some more ideas on crafting.

Homemade is very definitely hygge, from food to décor to gifts to socks and scarves. Yes, it takes money to garner the supplies, but it is far less expensive to cook a homemade meal for four than it is to buy it! The same is true for decorative items and well-crafted gifts. Besides, a beautiful hand-drawn card is a keepsake, not just another throwaway for the landfill. You can also customize cheaper store-bought items for a personal touch either for your home or as a gift: throw pillows, cushions, blankets can all easily be gussied up with your own personal style. Learn to knit (or invest in a cheater kit), as yarn and knitting needles are far less expensive than buying scarves and hats and so on.

Even if you aren't a very crafty person, you can still write a letter or send a thank you note. Gratitude is at the core of the hygge way of life, as well, and taking time out of your day for thanks is a frugal way to add some goodness to the world. Remember reading: talk about a frugal hygge thrill. Check out books from the library or scour used bookshops to buy plenty of fun and interesting reads. Encourage your friends to borrow and exchange books to widen your repertoire, as well. Start a book club and invite members to your warm and cozy house to talk books and sip mulled wine in front of the hearth.

Take stock of what you need rather than what you desire. Hygge is about returning to simple values and simple pleasures, and we all get caught up in the constant striving of consumer culture at times. One of the most frugal activities you can do is to take inventory of what you have and how much of it you use. It won't take long for you to begin to clearly decide what is necessary and what is clutter. In addition, this gives you the opportunity to re-purpose certain items that you have. As the cliché goes: "One man's trash is another man's treasure." You might find hidden treasures stuffed in the back of your closet. With a little housecleaning effort, you may be able to hygge up your house with virtually no additional expenditure.

Short of that, seek out used items for your hygge needs. Thrift stores and online warehouses offer lots of very affordable items, from comfy sweaters to great reads to household goods. For larger items, such as sofas or other furniture, Craigslist is always a solid option. In fact, the idea of recycling, of avoiding waste is central to the hygge philosophy and Scandinavian society in general.

Start a savings account: if you discover that you lack several things that you'd like to have to refine your hygge lifestyle, or if you're just starting out, then start a hygge account for those things. Putting aside a bit from each paycheck will allow you to afford pieces little by little. Having a savings account is a pretty good idea, anyway.

Also, remember that you don't have to do everything all at once. Start with one area of your life or home to begin practicing hygge. If you have a bike, then bike to the park - that's a start. If you want to start having friends over for game nights, then hygge up your living room - bedrooms and baths and wardrobe can wait. Take it one piece at a time, and remind yourself that hygge is a mindset, really, not a bunch of material things.

The simple things are often the best things in life, as well. It doesn't cost anything to spend some time snuggling with a loved one or looking through old pictures for a reminiscence costs absolutely nothing and means just about everything. Spending time with loved ones is infinitely better than spending money.

Chapter 10: Practical Hygge: Hygge Crafts

As has been mentioned frequently throughout the book, homemade and hand-crafted are most certainly at the heart of hygge practice. Not only does this encapsulate the spirit of the simple, slowed-down lifestyle, it also emphasizes both frugality and generosity. The frugality of crafting items from raw materials - always cheaper than buying mass-produced, factory-made goods - balanced with the expression of heartfelt generosity that is embodied in each handmade item you create is one of the deepest hallmarks of hygge practice. A handmade card with a thoughtful personal note is infinitely more hygge than a department store purchase; A lovely centerpiece made from found objects and natural materials is stunning in a way that a bought showpiece can never be. Wearing hats, scarves, and sweaters knitted by hand showcases the essence of hygge practice - cozy and caring, comfortable and generous. Happiness is but a quiet moment of thoughtful labor and an enduring satisfaction at creating joy for yourself and others with your own two hands.

Some general ideas of what kind of crafts are especially hygge follow, along with some specific suggestions for projects you could undertake in the Checklist section.

Remember that one of the key components to crafting in a hyggelige way is to savor the process. Sit back in your hyggekrog and relax into the gentle labors of knitting a quilt or stitching a sweater - or any other of the craft ideas to follow. Take pleasure in the soothing process of slowing down and embracing a task that our busy world has nearly forgotten. The end results are nothing short of the physical embodiment of the cozy, happy spirit of hygge.

When embarking on household projects - especially if you are new to the concept of crafting - think small and manageable. Instead of starting out knitting a sweater, think about adding some texture to a sweater or cardigan you already have. Adding texture to household items or wardrobe pieces is another hallmark of hygge. Learning to stitch a small but meaningful decoration on a beloved sweater is a way to accomplish both textural interest and the hyggelige joys of the homemade and personal.

Don't get bogged down in the big things, especially when it comes to hygge-fying your household. It may feel overwhelming to add large pieces of furniture, create a fireplace and hearth where none existed before, or to repaint a room or replace carpet. Those are big - *and sometimes expensive* – undertakings! In hygge, it's the little things that matter, the small and simple things that add spark to your home. A hand-painted vase or paper-made baubles, a decorative wreath made of natural materials or a small sampler for a throw pillow: these are the things that make your home cozy, comfortable, and meaningful.

Think of practicing crafting as expanding the hygge tenant of fostering relationships: handmade gifts are ever-so-thoughtful and warm the hearts of both the giver and the recipient. Even if you purchase a present for someone, you can personalize it with a handmade card or a cross-stitch tag. It is the little touches that can ultimately make the difference between a mediocre and memorable gift.

While we don't always associate the art of cooking as a craft, it most certainly is! Even though a culinary gift may be ephemeral, it is truly from the heart. The breaking of bread together is one of the most ancient and revered of all social interactions, and feeding people is expressing love in the most intimate of ways. Baking bread for a neighbor or friend - providing a handwritten recipe card with it - is one of the most hygge crafts in which you can indulge. At the holidays, baking of all types is a lovely way to spend a cold winter morning, while having the added satisfaction of providing cheerful - and yummy - sustenance to family and friends. A festive bag of various holiday cookies is a present par excellence.

Remember those candles? So important to hygge, candles and candlelight are at the very root of how to hygge in your home - and, *they can also be handmade.* For just a small initial investment in materials, you can customize candles - size, shape, scent - for yourself and your family and friends. It's also another element of the frugal nature of hygge, as homemade candles, in the long run, are less expensive than buying them, and recycling all the bits of wax left at the end of a candle's life leaves you with material to begin again!

Another craft idea that has been mentioned throughout the book is using natural materials in your household décor. It can be as simple as layering items in a clear jar or vase or as complicated as creating a pattern out of dried flowers to decorate a gift box. You can also adorn your table with a centerpiece or your mantle with a garland of natural materials. Even high-end restaurants are getting in on this trend, festooning walls and arches with actual organic material. There are abundant ideas to be had all over the internet, as well as books specializing in crafting from nature.

Certainly, as mentioned above, knitting is one of the central crafts to utilize the hygge spirit. It combines the use of soft, neutral materials with the ability to customize coziness via hats or scarves, sweaters, and afghans. While knitting is a skill that takes time to develop, there are some shortcut methods if you are a beginner. Weaving looms assist in doing the knitting for you. Consider embarking on smaller projects as you begin your hygge journey. While hygge may seem to call for the more traditional method, it certainly wouldn't forbid the beginner's learning curve. Even with the shortcut methods, there is the time spent in slowing down and creating with your hands.

While many crafts are instinctual and improvisational, there are innumerable resources out there for you. Even the most experienced crafter can glean new ideas and hone old skills by picking up a well-respected book on crafting the hygge way.

The Checklist

Here are some specific ideas for actual crafting projects that you could undertake, from knitting, crocheting, and sewing to home décor and miscellaneous other ideas. These projects range from ideas for the advanced crafter to simple tasks for beginners. Read through the entire list for a variety of ideas. Don't hesitate! Get started on one of these immensely satisfying projects today.

Pick out a knitting pattern for a hygge-style sweater. These patterns can be found in any local crafts store or in various places throughout the internet. Remember: a hand-knitted sweater isn't just a one-time gift, it's a precious keepsake to be passed down through the family.

Looking for something simpler than a sweater? Pick out a knitting pattern for a plush hand-knit bag - perhaps the perfect place to keep your knitting materials all in one cozy place when you're done. This would also be a terrific gift for a knitting friend, or it could be a cute accessory for a crisp winter day.

Or, you could tackle a quilting or blanket project. These patterns come available in the incredibly simple to incredibly complex: a cozy, chunky-knit afghan is possible to make in one mere day with some of these patterns. More complex items use a variety of materials, creating varying patterns and textures.

Crocheting is another nearly lost art that creates the same cozy, comfy feel of knitting for a variety of projects. For example, crochet yourself (or a loved one) some warm slippers for wearing while reading a book by the fire.

Or, you could crochet lovely cozies for your soup bowls or teapot or favorite mug. These custom-made cozies are guaranteed not only to keep your food and drink warm but also to make them aesthetically inviting. Practical and pretty, these are good project ideas for the beginning crochet aficionado.

You can also use your crochet skills to make small handbags or clutches, creating tapestry-like patterns to make another practical and pretty item for your personal use.

Pick out the very softest of yarns to crochet the ultimate scarf, the kind you'd like to nuzzle your face and hands into on the coldest of winter days. This is also a lovely gift idea for any friend or family member who enjoys the comforts of hygge.

Since you're starting to get into the whole idea of crafting, why not crochet yourself a personalized pincushion to help with your pins and such while sewing? It's a small but meaningful project that will keep you coming back to your crafting for more, simply because it's an inviting symbol of accomplishment.

There are also more complicated crocheting projects you can take on, such as crocheting an oversize poncho for use at the campfire, making it out of lighter material for the perfect accompaniment to an early spring picnic. Nice, chunky boot slippers are another way to hygge up your wardrobe via your own craftiness and don't forget the absolute usefulness of a lovely, handmade hat. Simple as they are, you can craft a hat for nearly every occasion.

Don't forget about one of the other essential parts of your hygge wardrobe and sew yourself up a pair of comfy sweatpants. There are some relatively easy patterns out there for you to follow. Short of sewing a pair, embroider your own favorite pair with a lovely design or meaningful phrase.

You could also apply sewing skills to other home items, such as pillowcases and decorative throws. Sewing a personal slipcover for a piece of furniture is also a nice project, as is creating personalized table linens, such as tablecloths, placemats, and napkins, either via adding decorative details or creating from scratch.

Don't forget the quilting tradition: save bits of this and that, things that have personal meaning and importance, to create a keepsake for the ages. Involve your friends, too, for a very hyggelige quilting circle.

There is also a northern tradition in the Scandinavian heart: these handmade hearts are made all over Scandinavia, sometimes a tradition attributed to the Danish author Hans Christian Andersen. These are particularly popular at Christmas. Often, they are very simple hearts made of paper, but the woven heart has a great following, as well. Making a few dozen of these to accompany packages at the holidays is a lovely way to start your own yearly tradition. Some specific ideas for home décor could include the following projects:

Use found pine cones to create a wreath. This could be crafted to hang on the wall or to serve as a centerpiece. With some consideration (i.e., avoid any fire danger), it could serve as a nest for a candle, as well.

Make some candles, as mentioned above. Remember that you need barely invest anything in materials: save up bits of wax from various spent candles and repurpose them in a teacup for a whole new look.

Make candle holders out of recycled and/or rustic materials. Burlap is an excellent material for this, for one example. Candle cozies have the additional benefit of muting the candle's glow for an even more hyggelige atmosphere, as well as adding a personal touch to your household décor.

How do you store all those mugs you've collected for coffee, cocoa, and tea? You make a stand or a wall hook out of wood. Hang your mugs from a hand-crafted, wooden project for both practical purposes - they're all right there at your fingertips - and artful display.

Speaking of displays, if you have the woodworking skills to craft these small projects, think of other places where you can put your crafting to both practical and pretty use. Consider crafting a mounted set of wall hooks for visitors to hang their coats and sweaters on, or a wooden tree or mount upon which to hang your jewelry in your bedroom. How about a simple box in which to store utensils or crafting materials? Just because something is practical doesn't suggest it shouldn't be meaningful.

Make wall hangings out of natural materials. Your sewing, knitting, or crocheting skills could come in handy here, or you could seek out various pieces in the remainder bin at your local craft store, pulling together something unique and personal. Bits of fur, swatches of various materials, even repurposed clothing can be stitched together to bring a bit of hygge style to your home. Be sure to focus on neutral, calming colors for the more hyggelige look, rather than a riot of a mismatch.

Make or customize your own photo frames. Using natural materials, you can craft your own frames for display throughout your house. This also makes for a wonderful gift. You could also customize frames by adding a bit of found natural material here and there - pick up and polish some sticks or stones in your own back yard - for something lovely and worthy of displaying your legacy.

Don't forget about the seasons! Homemade Christmas ornaments are a wonderful addition to any tree, from small stained-glass projects to painted baubles to crocheted garland. All these things create a very hygge holiday. Make a winter village to display throughout the season, from clay and paint. Attend a pottery workshop to craft some holiday candle holders or vases, and so on. Craft a handmade advent calendar to count down the days until Christmas. Write your best holiday recipes on lovely notecards to give to friends and family. Knit or crochet stockings for the family or embroider stockings you already have with names or sayings of holiday cheer. Truly, the ideas are infinite, and there are innumerable books and guides available for you to find the perfect craft to round out your hygge holiday experience.

Making a personalized scrapbook became a booming business about twenty years ago, and it remains a wonderful way for the beginning crafter to express love and gratitude toward family and friends. A fun way to think about scrapbooking is to tell a story using words, pictures, and decorative additions. Give your best friend a scrapbook for her 40th birthday or make a scrapbook to be completed for a mother-to-be or put together a scrapbook of inspirational sayings and images for an anniversary present or a college graduation gift. The possibilities are numerous and require minimal skill, just thoughtfulness and time.

Essential oils are another hyggelige way that you can personalize your home. Another "craft" that takes minimal skill and only a few materials, you can create your own scents and diffusers to place strategically throughout the house.

Speaking of scents, there are numerous crafty ideas to both decorate and aromatize your homes, such as drying herbs and/or flowers to be used in sachets for closets or drawers.

Remember: mugs, tableware, and other household items can be homemade or customized, as well. There are classes available in many places that offer instruction on pottery and amateur glassmaking, as well as woodworking and metalworking. Some of these are quite advanced, but there is also any number of beginner's projects to tackle at first.

Kitchen projects are another type of hygge crafting. Those going beyond the daily task of family meal making are especially in tune with the notion that homemade is better, engendering a greater spirit of generosity and a warm feeling of happiness. This feeling is for us, as givers, as much as for the recipients. Some potential projects and specific ideas to consider are as follows.

Canning: This is an ideal hyggelige craft if you have an abundant garden. This is not only a way to preserve your harvest, minimizing waste and maximizing frugality, but also a way to turn a glut of produce into a wonderful holiday gift. Think preserves and jams, pickles and sauces. A nearly foolproof way to preserve your harvest for months - even years - to come, canning is a lost art among most home cooks. Supermarkets have made it far too easy to obtain whatever produce you want at whatever time of year you desire it. While there is nothing inherently wrong with this, it's certainly economically and environmentally sound to grow your own food and to preserve it. Canning is a time-honored way to do just that.

Freezing: if you don't have the time or space for the equipment required in canning, you can put your freezer to good use. While this may not be the ideal way to plan on future gift-giving, it is undoubtedly a lovely gift to give yourself and your family: thawing a bag of homemade tomato sauce in the depths of February is like unleashing a ray of sunshine. If you want to make it even simpler than sauce, simply roast some of your abundant tomatoes for a few minutes in a hot oven, then slip off the peels and toss them into a - carefully labeled - freezer bag. Then, throughout the non-growing season, you can pull these out and use them however you wish. Other good candidates for freezing are any abundant vegetables from your garden or local farmer's market that can be blanched quickly, laid out on cookie sheets to freeze individually, then stored in freezer bags for the winter: think green beans, sugar snap peas, asparagus, broccoli, and cauliflower. Again, this is a way to treat yourself to some lovely and healthy self-care during the non-growing season.

Dehydrating is another way to preserve the produce of spring and summer, as well as having the side benefit of creating crafty ways to either scent or decorate your home. For example, if you end up with a glut of herbs, dehydrating these for future use is one of the best ways to use them up - and they smell lovely, as well, to add to a sachet or aromatic diffuser. For another example, if you have a glut of peppers, you can string these up on a *ristra* (or wreath) to dry. Not only can you use them in stews, soups, or sauces (or grind them for seasoning), but they also look beautiful in the kitchen.

Pickling: a time-honored tradition of home cooks everywhere, homemade pickles make lovely gifts and thrifty projects. Fermented foods have made a comeback in recent years as the growing consensus suggests that the active cultures (or probiotics) in naturally fermented foods are remarkably good for our overall health, especially in maintaining a healthy digestive system. Pickles that you buy in the supermarket are typically heat-treated in some way or pickled using vinegar and not fermentation; both methods effectively kill any active microorganisms. Naturally fermented or "pickled" vegetables made at home contain a host of good probiotics if monitored carefully and taste superior to mass-produced items.

There are other ways of using the kitchen as a craft center: making scented oils or vinegar for your own use or for gifts is a lovely way to customize a neutral oil. Use citrus peel and herbs, or garlic and spices for inspiration. Vinegar is especially good vehicles for infusing herbal essences, tarragon vinegar being a traditional condiment all over Europe. Don't forget the potent powers of alcohol, as well: distilling spirits at home isn't feasible, of course, but infusing neutral alcohol (usually vodka) with various flavors makes for a festive gift. Vanilla beans, citrus peels, peppercorns, and other aromatics make excellent candidates for a winter treat. You can also make your own liqueurs with various flavorings, some alcohol, and a bit of sugar. Homemade limoncello is easy, as is cinnamon or coffee liqueur. Make a big vat of mulled wine while you're at it, and seal into bottles with specialized labels to hand out to guests over the holidays. The kitchen is an ideal place to hone your hygge crafting abilities.

Finally, it would do us good to remember that the spirit of hygge suggests that we take delight in every day, in the simple things, so that the very mundane tasks with which our lives are filled should give us cause for joy and a pause for gratitude. In that sense, cleaning and caring for loved ones, doing laundry or mowing the land, are crafts of daily love and comforting happiness.

Conclusion

The art of hygge is a simple one: immerse yourself in the warmth and comfort of your beautifully lit and naturally decorated house with good friends, hearty food, and some happy conversation. Ride your bike to the local café for some coffee and fika. Indulge in some serene self-care, curled up in your cozy nook with a good book and a warm drink. Hygge is about fostering a long-term sense of happiness and general well-being; material consumption and ambitious striving are ephemeral distractions that lead us not to happiness - but to hurriedness. Hygge gives us the opportunity to step back from our overly busy lives and instead, start to value the small, daily joys that we are surrounded by. It encourages us to be present in our own lives.

Philosophically speaking, hygge is about comfort and coziness, preferably in the spirit of fellowship and family. Practically speaking, hygge is about designing a lifestyle that is simple and serene, warm and happy.

With all the practical tips and ideas that you have discovered throughout this book, you should be able to devise a hygge lifestyle that both comforts you and keeps you happy. From the atmosphere within your home to the clothing you choose to wear, you can embrace all aspects of hygge. Strike up a fire, start up a slow-simmered stew, stir up a warm and soothing drink, and be sure to invite some friends! Hygge is more than a trend or a hard-to-pronounce word; it is an immensely satisfying way of life that has engendered the happiness of millions. Now you can count yourself one of them.

Made in the USA
Columbia, SC
28 December 2022

75118427R00064